D0862101

BB

France:
Summer
1940

John Williams

Editor-in-Chief: Barrie Pitt
Art Director: Peter Dunbar

Military Consultant: Sir Basil Liddell Hart
Picture Editor: Bobby Hunt

Executive Editor: David Mason
Designer: Sarah Kingham
Cover: Denis Piper
Research Assistant: Yvonne Marsh
Cartographer: Richard Natkiel
Special Drawings: John Batchelor

Photographs for this book were especially selected from the following Archives: from left to right page 2-3
Suddeutscher Verlag; 6-7 Sudd. Verlag; 8-9 Ullstein; 10 Roger Viollet; 12 Ullstein; 13 Bibliothek fur
Zeitgeschiche; 16-17 Sudd. Verlag; 18-19 Sudd. Verlag; 21 Bundesarchiv; 22 Bibliothek fur Zeitgeschiche;
23 Sudd. Verlag; 24 Bibliothek fur Zeitgeschiche; 25 Roger Viollet; 28-29 Ullstein; 30 Imperial War Museum;
31 Ullstein; 32-33 Sudd. Verlag/Bibliothek fur Zeitgeschiche; 34-35 Ullstein; 39 Ullstein; 40-41 Ullstein;
42-43 Bibliothek fur Zeitgeschiche; 45 IWM; 48-49 IWM; 52-53 Bibliothek fur Zeitgeschiche; 55 Bibliothek fur
Zeitgeschiche; 56-57 Sudd. Verlag; 58 Ullstein; 60-61 IWM; 61 Bibliothek fur Zeitgeschiche; 66 Bibliothek fur
Zeitgeschiche; 66-67 Ullstein; 67 Sudd. Verlag; 68-69 IWM; 71 Documentation Tallandier; 74 Ullstein; 76 IWM/
Sudd. Verlag; 77 Sudd. Verlag; 79 Bibliothek fur Zeitgeschiche; 80-81 IWM; 83 IWM; 86-87 Bibliothek fur
Zeitgeschiche; 88-89 Sudd. Verlag; 90-91 IWM; 94 IWM; 96-97 Sudd. Verlag; 99 Documentation Tallandier;
100-101 Documentation Tallandier; 102-103 Staatsbibliothek Berlin; 104 IWM; 106 Sudd. Verlag; 107 Sudd.
Verlag; 109 IWM; 110-111 IWM/Sudd. Verlag; 116-117 Ullstein; 118 Bibliothek fur Zeitgeschiche; 119 Sudd.
Verlag/IWM; 120-121 Ullstein; 122 Bibliothek fur Zeitgeschiche; 123 Bibliothek fur Zeitgeschiche;
124 Bibliothek fur Zeitgeschiche; 124-125 Bibliothek fur Zeitgeschiche; 126 IWM; 128-129 Bibliothek fur
Zeitgeschiche; 130-131 Bibliothek fur Zeitgeschiche; 132 IWM; 133 Keystone; 136-137 Sudd. Verlag; 138
Bibliothek fur Zeitgeschiche; 140 Ullstein; 141 Sudd. Verlag; 142 Ullstein; 143 Bibliothek fur Zeitgeschiche
144-145 Ullstein; 147 Sudd. Verlag; 149 Bibliothek fur Zeitgeschiche; 151 Ullstein; 154 Documentation
Tallandier; 156 Ullstein; 157 Sudd. Verlag; 159 Sudd. Verlag.

Ballantine Books Inc.
101 Fifth Avenue New York NY 10003
An Intext Publisher

Contents

10⁰⁰

Out of Print

*68
wwⅡ*

The easiest victory in history

Introduction by Captain Sir Basil Liddell Hart

The fall of France took place within barely six weeks of the launching of the German offensive in the West on 10th May 1940 – and the issue was really decided in the first six days. It resulted in the war lasting six years and spreading over the world, with far-reaching effect on myriads of people, and appalling consequences to many millions of them.

Yet Germany's initial success was far from being inevitable, although it looked so after the event. Indeed, it could easily have been prevented.

It is far from true that Germany's victory was gained by an overwhelming superiority of force. She did not mobilise as many men as her opponents did – at the expense of their arms production The Germans managed to form and equip more divisions that the French did, but had no advantage in numbers over the total array of opposing divisions in the West. That did not matter. For the issue was really decided by the deep-driven thrusts of a picked eight percent of their army – their ten

armoured divisions – before the bulk had come into action.

This was not due to the German Army having a much greater number of tanks, as was naturally imagined at the time. Whereas the French estimated that it had 7,000–8,000 tanks, we now know that it had less than half this number – and less than 2,600 were used in the first, and decisive, phase of the invasion. The French had many more tanks, but they were not so mobile and the greater part of them were scattered as small packets, instead of being concentrated for a powerful punch. The French generals still clung to the 1918 idea that tanks were the servants of the infantry, while Hitler had listened to Guderian, the leader of the new school, who argued that armoured division should be the spearhead of the army.

Likewise, Hitler had gone all out for air power. Here he did have a big superiority in numbers, approaching 3 to 1, and he scored most heavily through having developed a mass of dive-bombers to combine with his

tanks. The French military chiefs had
tended to underrate the value of air-
power until it was too late to remedy
their prolonged neglect of the air arm.

Once across the Meuse, the tanks
bowled along the roads that led west,
meeting scarcely any opposition. In a
week they reached the Channel coast,
160 miles distant – and cut off the
Allied armies in Belgium. 'Dunkirk'
and the fall of France were the sequels.
It was the easiest-won victory in
history.

One reason was that the pace of
panzer warfare paralysed the French
Staff, whose minds were still moving
at 1918 tempo. The orders they issued
might have been effective but for
being, repeatedly, twenty-four hours
late for the situation they were
intended to meet.

Another reason was that the French
Staff were always trying to mount
massive counter-attacks, instead of
hurrying to man the stop-lines. Time
after time the Germans drove over
these lines, while the French reserves
were gradually assembling on the

flank. The French Staff were too
content to follow an old offensive
theory regardless of what was happening in practice.

The statesmen of France and Britain
had smoothed Hitler's path by failing
to see where their policy was leading.
The soldiers were equally short-
sighted in their sphere. The breakdown
of 1940 was basically due to the way
that military orthodoxy prevailed
over modern ideas, not only at that
moment, but for twenty years before.
The French and British – except for
the small band of modern thinkers
who preached the idea of mobile-
mechanised warfare – had been pre-
ponderantly conservative ever since
their victory in 1918, whereas the
Germans had been spurred by their
defeat in 1918 to become relatively
progressive. There is the key to what
happened on the battlefields of 1940.

In this book, John Williams clears
away many myths, providing an able
and illuminating account, a study in
depth, of the dramatic and fateful
events of 1940.

The rival plans

In the still, clear dawn of Friday, 10th May 1940, the massed forces of Hitler's Germany irrupted across the borders of Holland, Belgium and Luxembourg, to end the long inertia of the 'phoney war' which apart from the invasion of Norway and Denmark a month earlier, had persisted since the outbreak of the Second World War the previous September. It was the beginning of the great Battle of the West.

In France there was no invasion as yet: the attacks were confined to bombing raids deep into French territory. At Supreme Headquarters, Vincennes, just east of Paris, reports of enemy activity had been coming in since 1 am; and five hours later, when there was no longer any possibility of a false alarm, General Gamelin, Allied Commander-in-Chief, issued from his office in the gloomy casemates of Vincennes the historic order 'Holland-Belgium manoeuvre Dyle' which was to set in motion the great forward wheel of the Franco-British armies to their pre-arranged Dutch and Belgian battle positions.

Now that the moment had come, 67-year-old General Maurice Gamelin – known for his imperturbability – appeared remarkably confident. A staff officer arriving at Vincennes had never seen him so buoyant. Short and sturdy, the general was walking the headquarters corridor 'quietly humming a martial air'. Before the sun was well up that morning he expressed his optimism to his troops in his first Order of the Day: 'The attack which we have foreseen since October has been launched this morning. Germany is opening against us a struggle to the death. The watchword for France and her Allies is: "Courage, energy, confidence." As Marshal Pétain said twenty-four years ago: *"Nous les aurons* (We shall get them)".'

'Courage, energy, confidence' was a fine battle-cry, and no doubt the prospect of action, after months of tedium and waiting, was a tonic to the morale of the French and British as they prepared to move north to engage the enemy. But as the formidable German war-machine surged over the Dutch, Belgian and Luxembourg frontiers in

those early hours of the 10th May, what exactly was the strategic plan to which the Allied armies were committed?

Since September 1939 the Allied (Franco-British) General Staffs had perfected a scheme known as Plan D or the Dyle Plan (after the Belgian river Dyle). Framed on the supposition that the Germans would, as in 1914, advance through Belgium when they attacked in the West, the plan specified, as a counter to this move, a Franco-British advance from the French frontier into Belgium, to occupy a line based on the river Dyle. The planners were handicapped by the strictly neutral attitude of the Belgians (and Dutch) which precluded the entry of Allied troops into their territory before a German attack. Nevertheless in its final form Plan D allowed for such entry to both countries and was agreed as follows.

From south to north five armies would be involved – the French Ninth Army, the French First Army, the British Expeditionary Force, the Belgian Army itself, and the French Seventh Army (which would occupy the Breda-St Leonard line across the Dutch frontier). After an initial German attack these forces would take up the following positions (the Belgians would already be *in situ*) from south to north: French Ninth Army, Mézières-Namur; French First Army, Namur-Wavre; BEF, Wavre-Louvain; Belgian Army, Louvain-Antwerp; French Seventh Army, Turnhout-Breda. (North of the Seventh Army, Holland would be covered by the Dutch Army.) Thus, along with the Belgian Army, one British and three French armies would confront the Germans on a one hundred mile line, based on river barriers and strengthened with fortifications, across the length of Belgium and into Holland.

In shaping Plan D the planners had assumed that the main German as-

The ground troops prepare their advance into France

9

sault would be delivered in the Belgian plains north of Namur. They had dismissed the region south of Namur – the rugged forest country of the Ardennes and the steep-banked Meuse – as offering no serious threat. 'This sector is not dangerous,' Marshal Pétain had told an Army Commission in 1934. As a logical outcome of this thinking, the Plan D decision – so fateful for the Allies – was made to place the two strongest French armies, the Seventh and First, north of Namur, and the weakest to the south.

Meanwhile, in the months of uneasy truce in the West, Hitler had been making his own plans. The original German invasion scheme had in fact been for an outflanking movement through central Belgium (on the lines of the 1914 Schlieffen Plan), as laid down in the first version of the German Plan Yellow, produced in mid-October 1939. This specified a subsidiary operation through the Ardennes. But one German general, Erich von Manstein – Chief of Staff to General von Rundstedt, commander of Army Group A, the group detailed for the Ardennes action – did not approve the plan. Foreseeing that central Belgium would be heavily defended, his own idea was for the main assault to be made by Army Group A in the more lightly protected Ardennes-Meuse sector. But was the notoriously difficult Ardennes terrain negotiable by tanks? On this question Manstein consulted the tank expert General Heinz Guderian who, after careful study, pronounced the operation practicable.

Rundstedt himself now took up the proposal, and he and Manstein strongly recommended it to the OKH (German Army High Command), but without success. The idea would have foundered altogether had not Manstein – posted elsewhere because he had become a nuisance to OKH –

General Maurice Gamelin, Allied Commander-in-Chief

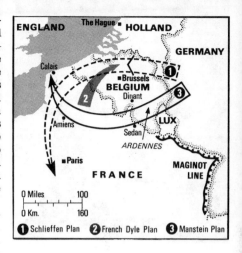

1 Schlieffen Plan　2 French Dyle Plan　3 Manstein Plan

happened in February to dine with Hitler, to whom he explained his plan. The Führer, dubious about the original scheme, partly because it had been revealed to the Allies through German plans captured in Belgium in January, was much impressed and at once adopted Manstein's Ardennes plan, incorporating it in his War Directive No 10 of 18th February 1940. A week later Plan Yellow, in its fifth and final form, was issued. This gave Rundstedt's Army Group A the chief role in the coming offensive. Increased to forty-four divisions, of which seven were armoured, the group was to traverse the Ardennes and cross the Meuse between Sedan (in France) and Dinant (in Belgium) and establish bridgeheads with the aim of advancing towards the Channel. Opposing this massive force, as already noted, would be the weakest of the French armies. Thus by a fateful play of destiny – or brilliant thinking on Manstein's part – were the French planners outplanned and the trapping in Belgium of a large part of the Allied armies virtually assured before ever the offensive had begun.

But other factors too were operating against France on this crucial 10th May. Though physically mobilised for war, she lacked the national

11

unity and steely determination necessary for the all-out struggle that faced her. Moreover, the long truce of the 'phoney war' had served to dissipate whatever sense of urgency had possessed her in September 1939 – perhaps had even bred a mood of false optimism and over-confidence. But behind this lay a deep aversion to war, bred of her long-standing conflict with her old enemy and more powerful neighbour, Germany.

Defeated in the Franco-Prussian War of 1870 and suffering crippling casualties and vast damage at Germany's hands in the First World War, France had since then sought security above all, a security that had expressed itself militarily in a defensive strategy and the building of the great Maginot Line – the magic barrier that would keep out the German aggressor for ever.

The original thinking behind the Maginot Line had been sound. At the end of the First World War, France, in her determination never again to undergo invasion by Germany, had been faced with an additional defence problem: the protection of the newly recovered Alsace-Lorraine provinces, lost to her as a result of the 1870 war. This region was vital to France for its coal and potash; and if it were to avoid destruction in the event of a German attack it would have to be defended on the frontier. Pending the arrival of troops from the rear, the best means of immediate defence, it was argued, was a permanent fortified system. The scheme took its name from the wounded First World War veteran and man of Lorraine, André Maginot, who strongly mistrusted the notion of a peaceful Germany and who began his campaign for the provision of the Alsace-Lorraine defences as Minister of War in 1922. Throughout the 1920s he and his successor Paul Painlevé worked energetically to get his plan implemented, while the pundits of the General Staff pondered indecisively on the kind of defences to be built and the length to which they should extend.

Involved in the decision-making were France's two great First World War leaders, Marshals Joffre and Pétain, whose views on the matter clashed. Joffre (post-war President of the Commission for Fortified Areas) proposed a string of separate fortified zones from the North Sea to the Swiss border, between which full-scale assaults could be launched. On the other hand Pétain (Vice-President of the Army Council and Inspector-General of the Army) favoured an unbroken defensive system to protect the northeast frontier only. The scheme that, after much deliberation, was finally adopted in 1928 was a

Far left: General Eric von Manstein. *Left:* General Gerd von Rundstedt, Commander German Army Group A, which was detailed to attack through the Ardennes. *Above:* Hitler studies operational plans with service chiefs at his headquarters

compromise. Joffre's fortified regions were to be joined to Pétain's continuous defences in a system covering the Rhine and northeast. Thus with the 'offensive' concept ruled out and the defences unbroken, Pétain's ideas – putting defence above all other considerations – had prevailed.

Financial and other difficulties delayed the completion of the Maginot Line until 1938. France now had a great fortified steel-and-concrete bastion protecting (in varying depth and strength) her eastern and northeastern frontiers from Basel to Montmédy. It was never planned to extend the line farther west than Montmédy because, as it was alleged, the Franco-Belgian frontier was too near such vital centres as Lille, and the subsoil appeared unsuitable for massive concrete structures. Moreover, it was thought undesirable to offend Belgium by the building of fortifications which might imply that France would not move to Belgium's aid in the event of a German attack on Belgium.

However valid these factors, the basic weakness of the Maginot Line was now revealed. Finishing as it did

at Montmédy, it was a line that could be turned, 'a perilous open-ended commitment'. Furthermore, the Pétainist defensive strategy now appeared fundamentally inconsistent in that it had produced, from the Channel to Basel, a hybrid defence line, relying, along one part of its length, on static fortifications, and, along another part, on a troop mobility that would be effective only if it were spearheaded by the particular arm that Parliament and the General Staff had persistently rejected since it had been first proposed by a progressive professional soldier named Lieutenant-Colonel Charles de Gaulle in 1934 – the armoured formation. Instead of this arm, essential for the kind of warfare in which France was likely to be involved by an aggressive Germany, the French Army was preparing to use basically the same slow-moving infantry as in the First World War. In other words the French, whether or not they planned to advance beyond their frontier into Belgium to counter a German attack, were – in the sector from the Channel to Montmédy – committed to a war of movement for which they were

13

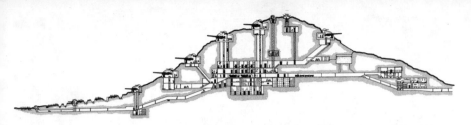

The Maginot Line was built during the 1930s, and took ten years to construct. Originally intended to defend only Alsace-Lorraine, it eventually stretched from Switzerland to Longuyon, where the Ardennes Forest begins. Against frontal attack the fortifications were presumed invincible, but they gave the French a false sense of security, a complacent attitude which critics dubbed the 'Maginot mentality'. Mobile defences based on armoured divisions and air power would have been more appropriate to modern conditions.

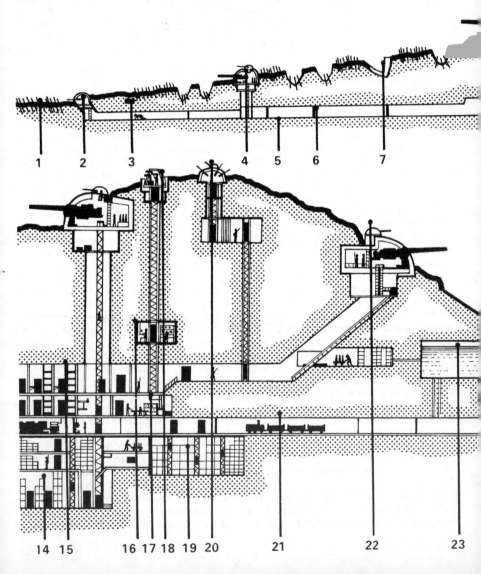

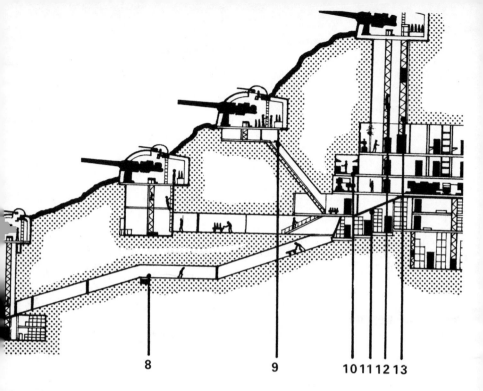

8   9   10 11 12 13

1. Tank trap. 2. Machine gun. 3. Mine. 4. Anti-tank and machine guns. 5. Emergency demolition mine. 6. Steel doors. 7. Infantry trap. 8. Emergency demolition mine. 9. Escalators. 10. Air conditioning plant and generators. 11. Stores. 12. Shell hoists. 13. Main lift. 14. Main magazine. 15. Barracks. 16. Telephones. 17. Main control room. 18. Main observation post. 19. Magazine. 20. Anti-aircraft machine guns. 21. Railway. 22. Machine gun posts on all guns. 23. Water supply. 24. Hospital. 25. Guardroom. 26. Rest quarters.

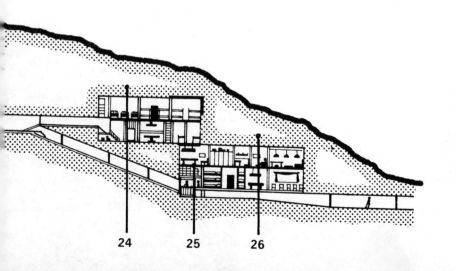

24   25   26

totally unequipped.

These were the strategic short-comings occasioned by France's dedication to passive defence and refusal to adopt modern offensive techniques. At the same time she was being beset by political troubles, denied the benefit of strong leadership and increasingly affected by a pacifist-defeatist mood. All this boded ill for her war-making capacity when she once more confronted Germany in September 1939.

Nevertheless her soldiers had answered the call-up with a certain grim sense of purpose. '*Il faut en finir* (We've got to finish it)' was the cry. The men were 'ready for heroism', wrote one newspaper correspondent, though not for bravado'. But unhappily for the morale of the French Army, instead of fighting, for eight months it was condemned to kick its heels in idleness and almost peacetime routine. Its fighting spirit was gradually eroded by absence of action, false hopes that perhaps Hitler never would attack, propaganda by pamphlet and loudspeaker from the German lines, even defeatist talk from the French rear.

On mobilization France's Field Army numbered 2,776,000 and her Army of the Interior 2,224,000. For the French High Command it was a problem how to employ these huge forces. The only possibilities were training and defence work; but these activities were badly hampered by the intense cold of the winter 1939–40. Another handicap was the poor morale and discipline of many older reservist troops (reservists formed four-fifths of the French Army). Moreover, regimental officers and NCOs often lacked authority or were insufficiently experienced. Senior officers, too, were wanting in drive and urgency. The defects even extended to Supreme Headquarters, where General Gamelin himself, as he confessed, was unaware of any weakness in the army.

Equally serious, in the 'phoney war' months, was the French neglect of the lessons of the recent Polish campaign, in which Germany had defeated Poland in less than a month. Though it was obvious from Poland that the tank now dominated the battlefield, the French High Command – in its pursuance of Plan D – was still allotting it a role secondary to the infantry. Thus, though tank production was to reach about 3,000 by May 1940 – approximately equalling the German output – the French tanks were ill-adapted for modern mobile warfare, being slow, heavy and unwieldy compared with the German tanks, which were lightly armoured and gunned and built primarily for speed and range. (According to the military historian Adolphe Goutard, *The Battle of France*, 1940, the main types of French tanks were the light-medium R35 and H35, the fast-medium Somua 36 and the heavy B1 and B2. Other types were the H39 and R40. The main German types were the panzer KwI, KwII, KwIII and KwIV.)

The French were also blind to the key offensive role, as demonstrated in Poland, of aircraft. Whereas Germany was to possess over 3,000 planes by May 1940, including up to 400 Stuka dive-bombers, France would dispose

some 1,200 – with no dive-bombers. This meant a German superiority of nearly three to one, though the rival fighting strength, if the 130 British fighter planes to be based in France in May 1940 were counted in, would be roughly equal – an Allied total of 800-odd compared with a German total of 1,000 at most. In speed, however, the Germans would hold the advantage, with their Messerschmitts (Me 109s and Me 110s) capable of some 360 mph as against the 306 mph of the French Curtiss, the 300 mph of the Potez and Morane, and the 356 mph of the French-based Hurricanes. In heavy and medium bomber strength France would be vastly inferior in May 1940: she would have a mere 150 against Germany's 1,470.

Her artillery position would be no better – fewer than 3,000 anti-aircraft guns compared with Germany's 9,300; and French anti-tank gun production, at no more than 8,000, was to be well below requirements. Only in field artillery – that arm in which she was famous – would France exceed Germany. By May she would dispose over 11,000 guns of all calibres from 75mm to 280mm, contrasted with Germany's 7,700-odd. But even this was no real advantage, for French artillery was mainly horse-drawn and thus unsuited to mobile operations.

It was in the face of all these shortcomings and deficiencies that General Gamelin contentedly hummed his martial air in the casemates of Vincennes early on 10th May. But if he was confident in France's military readiness, his Government was less than confident in him. Paul Reynaud, who had succeeded Edouard Daladier as Premier in March 1940, was profoundly dissatisfied with Gamelin's handling of the French part in the recent Allied expedition to Norway and had resolved to relieve him of his command. He put the matter to the Cabinet on 9th May – less than twenty-four hours before the German attack. The majority supported him, but Daladier, National Defence and War Minister, and Gamelin's firm friend, opposed him. In a crisis atmosphere, Reynaud decided to resign. On news of the German offensive he changed his mind and rescinded his objections to Gamelin. He sent the general a brief note: ' . . . Only one thing counts – to win the victory.' Gamelin replied: ' . . . France alone is of importance.'

German artillery on the Rhine, March

The Allies move north

Hitler opened his offensive on the Low Countries at approximately 4.30 am, with a devastating air attack on vital defence targets. After the bombs came the paratroops, dropped from Junkers 52 transports. Then followed the glider-borne units, racing to capture strategic airfields and bridges. At scores of points Dutch and Belgian defenders, though previously alerted, were overwhelmed by the speed and violence of the assault. And while this havoc was being created in the Dutch and Belgian rear, across some 270 miles of the frontiers of Holland, Belgium and Luxembourg rolled the leading formations of two German army groups – the great invasion force of Plan Yellow.

For his western offensive Hitler had assembled some 117 divisions, including an OKH reserve of about forty-two. He was thus allotting some seventy-five divisions to the assault on the Low Countries and Luxembourg. In the north General Fedor von Bock's Army Group B (the Eighteenth Army, General von Küchler, and Sixth Army, General von Reichenau) was heading into Holland,

and Belgium north of Liège, its role being to subdue Holland and contain the largest possible body of Allied troops in Belgium. South of Army Group B, General von Rundstedt's Army Group A (the Fourth Army, General von Kluge, supported by the Twelfth Army, General List, and Sixteenth Army, General Busch) was pushing into central Belgium and Luxembourg. Rundstedt's was the crucial role – to traverse the Ardennes, cross the Meuse and press westward through southern Belgium and northern France. Army Group A comprised forty-five divisions compared with Army Group B's twenty-eight.

Ahead of Rundstedt's infantry, grinding forward into Luxembourg's Ardennes forests, was the pride of Hitler's whole offensive, the armoured spearhead – no less than seven out of the German Army's total of ten Panzer divisions – that was to crash its way west between Dinant and Sedan and onwards to the Channel. This massed Panzer phalanx was concentrated in two formations, General von Kleist's group of five divisions

and General Hoth's group of two, attached to Kluge's Fourth Army command. Two of the remaining three armoured divisions, currently with Army Group B, were earmarked to supplement the southern striking force as occasion demanded. In all, Kluge's army was to dispose some 2,500 tanks.

But less significant than the number of German tanks was the way in which they were being employed. On the use of this mobile armoured weapon some of Germany's brightest military minds had been concentrating in the inter-war years while the French General Staff had been preoccupied with the building of the Maginot Line. Working on ideas propounded by the British experts Fuller, Liddell Hart and Martel, far-seeing German officers like Colonel (later General) Heinz Guderian perceived the enormous possibilities of the tank as the basis of a new kind of large-scale warfare. No longer would it be basically an infantry tool as in the First World War, but an arm in its own right, to be deployed in concentrated formation as an inde-

pendent armoured force, with a specifically offensive mission.

Guderian had been impressed by Liddell Hart's concept of the armoured division which would combine Panzer and Panzer-infantry units, and in the early twenties became keen to develop the notion for the use of the German Army. But capturing the interest of his superiors had been an uphill fight. After a successful theoretical exercise in 1929, using an imaginary armoured division, a senior general declared that tanks were 'a Utopian dream'. Not until Hitler's succession as Chancellor in 1933 was real progress made towards creating an armoured force. Then, following satisfactory experimental manoeuvres in summer 1935, three pioneer Panzer divisions – the 1st, 2nd and 3rd – were formed that October.

The German Panzer force was now accepted. Thenceforth, as it was expanded to its Second World War strength of ten divisions, appropriate tactics for the new arm were perfected. With their accompanying motorized divisions – and supported by bomber aircraft (a vital ancillary)

General Heinz Guderian, Commander, XIX Panzer Corps

General Fedor von Bock, Commander, Army Group B

– the Panzer formations were in fact to revolutionize warfare.

Their speed and mobility made them suitable for long-range thrusts and operations against the enemy's communications; and employed in sufficient concentrations, they were able to penetrate even a strong frontal position and advance swiftly beyond it before the defenders could close the breach. In forthcoming battles this was to be one of their vital roles, speed being always more important than fire-power. Exploitation, moreover, was to be in depth rather than laterally, the utmost reliance being placed on the *Luftwaffe*, whose Stuka dive-bombers would perform a preliminary 'softening-up'.

It was with this formidable arm – ironically, as first employed in concentrated offensive formation by the British at Cambrai in 1917 – that Germany now looked to repeat, against France, the spectacular defeat she had inflicted on Poland seven months earlier.

Meanwhile, General Gamelin's 'Dyle' order had gone down from Supreme Headquarters to the headquarters, at nearby La Ferté-sous-Jouarre on the Marne, of General Georges, Commander-in-Chief, North-east, who, under Gamelin, was responsible for directing operations, and thence to General Billotte, commanding 1st Army Group, the Allied force that was to move forward into Belgium. And soon after 7am 1st Army Group's advance formations – the 1st Light Mechanized Division of the French Seventh Army (General Giraud); the 2nd and 3rd Light Mechanized Divisions (General Prioux' Cavalry Corps) of the French First Army (General Blanchard); the vanguard divisions of the BEF's I and II Corps (Lord Gort); the leading units of the French Ninth Army (General Corap) – were preparing to head past the raised Belgian frontier barriers.

These formations had varying distances to travel. To reach the Dutch Belgian border, Giraud's Seventh Army had to cover over 100 miles; the BEF, allotted the seventeen-mile Louvain-Wavre sector, some seventy miles; Blanchard's First Army, assigned the twenty-five-mile Wavre-Namur sector, about fifty miles; Corap's Ninth Army merely had to pivot on a point somewhere north of Mézières and cover a fifty-mile front behind the French and Belgian Meuse extending north to Namur.

The only part of the Plan D line not

General Ewald von Kleist, Commander, Panzer Group Kleist

General Walter von Reichenau, Commander, German Sixth Army

covered by these Franco-British formations was the sector Antwerp-Louvain. This was the responsibility of the Belgians. The Belgian Army, commanded by Belgium's King, Leopold III, had a vital role to play in the Plan D strategy. With its flanks covered by the advance Franco-British formations, it would bear the main initial weight of the German attack until the whole Plan D line was manned. Of its total of twenty-four infantry divisions, ten were to hold the key defensive positions on the Albert Canal, the Meuse, and the fortified bases of Antwerp, Liège and Namur. Two forward divisions would man the frontier canals and two would operate in Belgian Limburg. One division would stay on the Antwerp-Louvain defence line, guarding Brussels, and the rest would be in reserve.

When the Franco-British formations were finally in their Plan D positions alongside the Belgians, the Allied forces deployed across Belgium and extending into Holland would total some fifty-three divisions – including, besides the ten divisions of the BEF, the best divisions of the French Army. While Corap's Ninth Army in the south was largely composed of poorish

reserve divisions, Blanchard's First Army comprised two light mechanized divisions, three 'active' or first-rate pre-war divisions and one 'Series A' or first reserve division, and Giraud's Seventh Army comprised one light mechanized division, two motorized infantry divisions, one 'active' one 'Series A' and two 'Series B' or second reserve divisions.

But not only was Gamelin, in the name of Plan C and on the firm assumption that the Germans would stage their main attack in central Belgium, sending the flower of his fighting formations right into Belgium and leaving the Meuse, where it ran from France into Belgium, to be guarded by his least reliable troops: he had placed, on Corap's right – along an important stretch of the French Meuse – an equally weak force, General Huntziger's Second Army. The French planners could not have made their dispositions more conveniently for the Germans if they had tried.

The French showed one other grave defect as they moved to battle on 10th May: they were deploying no armoured divisions. At the outbreak of war they had no armoured divisions at all. Not until January 1940 were the

21

Left: King Leopold of the Belgians, Commander-in-Chief of the Belgian Army. Above: General Hans von Kluge, Commander, German Fourth Army. Right: Hitler with German paratroops who captured the powerful Belgian fortress, Eben-Emael

1st and 2nd Divisions formed, and the 3rd even later. According to General Georges (C-in-C, Northeast), only the 1st Division was ready to fight on 10th May. With the unready 2nd and 3rd Armoured Divisions, this was now held in reserve. One further division, the 4th, was to be hastily created in the coming weeks. The extraordinary misuse of these armoured divisions – when they *were* finally employed – was to demonstrate the French failure to grasp the real purpose and potentialities of the tank as an offensive weapon.

While Holland and Belgium were now under full-scale attack, along the French frontier all was quiet. For the moment France was outside the ground-fighting zone. From the Western end of the Maginot Line near Montmédy, eastwards and then southwards to the Swiss border, four French armies (in 2nd and 3rd Army Groups commanded respectively by Generals Prételat and Besson) guard-ed the steel and concrete forts of France's great defensive bastion. Facing them were the First and Seventh Armies of General Ritter von Leeb's Army Group C. His seventeen divisions were immobilising more than thrice their number of French divisions, some at least of which, being 'active' divisions, might well have been of more use farther west, and in particular in the vulnerable Meuse sector, currently manned by the sixteen mediocre divisions of Corap's and Huntziger's Ninth and Second Armies.

In the battle-zone itself the early fighting was going badly for both Dutch and Belgians. Shaken and disrupted by the dawn assault, they were being heavily pressed at various points in front and rear. The Dutch under General Winkelmann were fal-ling back to the Maas (Dutch Meuse) and Upper Ýssel. More serious, in a retreat in the Maastricht peninsula

(the strip of Dutch territory separating Belgian Limburg from Germany) they had failed to destroy certain Maas bridges. The German seizure of these bridges was disastrous for the Belgians, for it enabled the enemy – who was concentrating the main weight of his attack on the peninsula – to turn the eastern end of the Albert Canal and cross the canal itself as well as the Maas. Meanwhile the key Belgian fort of Eben Emael, a few miles south near Liège, was under violent airborne attack.

Behind this forward line, a setback awaited the French. During the morning a First Army advance party reached its Plan D Wavre-Namur sector to find almost no defences, apparently because the Belgians had changed their minds about constructing anti-tank and other obstacles here and built them farther forward instead. The discovery was disconcerting, for this sector linking the

Dyle and Meuse river lines, included the hazardous 'Gembloux Gap', an area of open terrain notably favourable for tanks. Immediately to the north, advance units of the BEF were discovering a similar unpreparedness in the Louvain-Wavre sector.

The rapid German crossing of the Maas and the Albert Canal was to prove awkward for General Prioux' (First Army) Cavalry Corps when it took up its forward covering stations that afternoon on the line Tirlemont-Hannut-Huy. With no main French force behind him as yet and the Belgians being hard-pressed by Reichenau's sixth Army some thirty miles in front, he felt uncomfortably exposed. This risk pin-pointed the hazards attending Plan D on Day 1 of the battle: unless the Belgians could continue to hold the canal line for anything up to five days, while the Franco-British formations moved into position behind them, the success of

German troops advance in Belgium

the plan was jeopardised.

At the southernmost end of the great Allied wheeling manoeuvre, General Corap's Ninth Army, besides forming part of the defence line, had an important initial role. It was to send advance formations across the Meuse into the Belgian Ardennes to ascertain the strength of approaching enemy forces, and if necessary fight a delaying action while Corap's main body took post along the Belgian and French Meuse. But the Ninth was slow to start: its motorized units did not reach the Meuse until afternoon, thus losing valuable time on its vital mission. To the right of the Ninth, General Huntziger's Second Army (while basically performing the static role of guarding the Meuse's Sedan sector, it had an initial patrolling function like that of the Ninth) moved more promptly. Its scouting

units were crossing the Meuse by 7am.

In the nearby Belgian Ardennes, just over the river, the Belgians seemed unable to realise that the Germans had finally attacked. In the small holiday town of Bouillon they watched Huntziger's troops heading north with stares of amazement. That afternoon Bouillon's mayor listened astonished to a request by Huntziger himself for hospital accommodation. 'But, *mon général*,' he stammered, ' our hotels are reserved for tourists! Do you really think we are in any danger?'

The danger was real and not far distant. Forty miles east, General von Kleist's Panzers were already thrusting through the Belgian Ardennes. The five-division group was headed on the left by General Heinz Guderian's XIX Armoured Corps of three divisions moving in arrowhead formation: the 1st Panzer Division leading in the centre, the 10th on the left and the 2nd on the right. These were aiming for Sedan. Close behind them, on the right, came General Reinhardt's XLI Armoured Corps – the 6th and 8th Panzer Divisions and a motorized division – pointing towards Mézières (west of Sedan). To the right again came General Hoth's corps of the 5th and 7th Panzer Divisions and a motorized division, forging towards Dinant on the Belgian Meuse. With some 400 tanks to a division, this made a total of over 2,500 tanks. And supporting this massive armoured striking force were the thirty-seven infantry divisions of General von Rundstedt's Army Group A, behind which were poised the forty-two divisions of the German General Reserve.

There was no doubt about the boldness of this Ardennes move. The hilly, forested Ardennes, a region of plateaux, ridges, rocky ravines and narrow winding trails, its heathland interspersed with bog, had traditionally been avoided by armies whenever possible. It had, however, been negotiated by the Germans in the First World War, when their Fourth and Fifth Armies had, as part of the Schlieffen Plan, moved through it to attack and defeat the French. But that was with infantry: more hazardous was the committing of whole tank formations, and accompanying transport, to what was far from ideal tank country. But in favour of the daring project were two factors. One was the existence of a number of serviceable east-west roads, notably in the direction of Sedan and Rocroi (to Sedan's northwest). The other was the intensive training and rehearsal to which the shrewd and experience Guderian – Germany's foremost tank expert – had put his Panzer units, in a stretch of Germany territory comparable to the Ardennes, the hilly Eifel region between the Rhine and Moselle rivers.

It should, however, be noted that while the French General Staff –

Paul Reynaud, French Prime Minister

General Georges, C-in-C, North East

General Lord Gort

General Corap

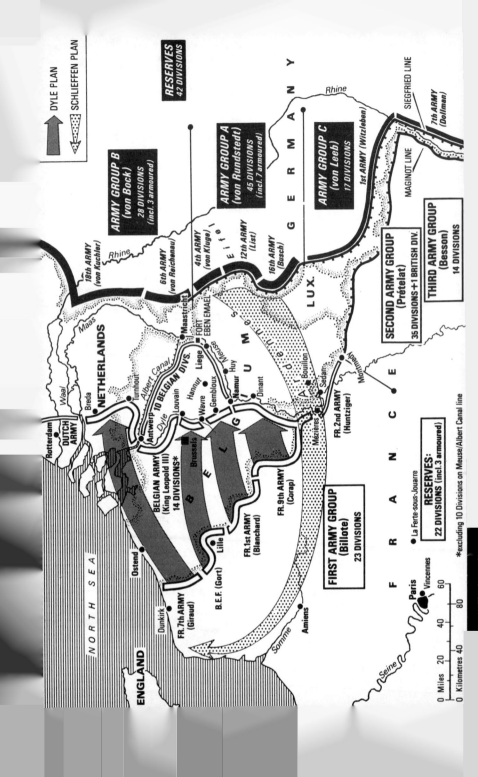

along with the British – had in the inter-war years dismissed the Ardennes as an unsuitable approach-route for advancing German armies, one British military expert, Captain BH (later Sir Basil) Liddell Hart, was expressing a different view. After touring the Ardennes in 1928 to study its potentialities, he wrote that in his opinion, the conclusions of the French and British were based on a delusion. Liddell Hart found the Ardennes in general well-roaded, and described most of it as rolling rather than mountainous country. The impassability of the Ardennes had, he judged, been 'much exaggerated'. Captain Liddell Hart made a further study of the Ardennes in 1938 which confirmed this estimate.

Quickly overcoming initial Belgian resistance and unmolested by a single Allied plane, the Germans met their first real opposition late that afternoon from Huntziger's advance forces (the 2nd Cavalry Division) around Arlon and Florenville, near the Franco-Belgian frontier. At dusk the French withdrew, somewhat mauled, to a line well back from the Bastogne-Arlon Line they had been ordered to reach. Farther north, Huntziger's 5th Cavalry Division had reached Libramont without seeing the enemy. But the 5th's left flank was now jeopardised by the failure of Corap's Ninth Army units to cross the Meuse on time. A sharp order went from General Georges at GHQ, Northeast, to Corap to hurry his forces across the river. But neither Georges nor his two army commanders recognised the formidable enemy threat building up under cover of the 'impenetrable' Ardennes. At Supreme Headquarters, Vincennes, General Gamelin was likewise unaware of the danger. Somewhat naturally, he was concentrating on Reichenau's expected assault in central Belgium. Throughout the morning he continued to be satisfied at the way things were going. As yet he saw nothing to shake his firm confidence in Plan D. But others were not so happy. One doubter was Paul Reynaud, who had never liked the strategic implications of Gamelin's plan. That morning he had said drily to Paul Baudouin, Secretary of the War Cabinet: 'Now Gamelin has the battle he has waited for . . . We shall see what he is worth.'

Vincennes was not the best place from which to assess the progress of the battle. The gloomy casemates that housed Supreme Headquarters seemed, under their frowning, nine-centuries-old pile that had been both palace and prison, remote from the actualities of modern war. The offices, unreached by daylight, had a stale depressing air. More significant, it was clear this day that Supreme Headquarters was out of touch operationally – being either denied a prompt service of information or bypassed altogether. This stemmed largely from Gamelin's anomalous status as Supreme Commander.

In addition to being Allied Commander-in-Chief he was France's Commander-in-Chief and National Defence Chief of Staff. But in fact, in the event of hostilities he had virtually no voice in directing operations. At Vincennes he headed an awkward tripartite command system which included GHQ Land Forces, at nearby Montry, and GHQ Northeast, at La Ferté-sous-Jouarre. This arrangement, the result of a recent reorganisation by himself, gave General Georges, at La Ferté, operational command, while Gamelin's Chief of Staff, General Doumenc, presided at Montry, being a kind of intermediary between Gamelin and Georges. The net result was that militarily the Supreme Commander was now little more than a figurehead. He was thus – as his staff uneasily noted on this Day 1 – not being fully informed of events. But the most glaring evidence of Vincennes' unimportance was its lack of a radio post. The Supreme Commander had no wireless communication with his armies.

Threat from the Ardennes

In Paris and elsewhere the French had greeted the news of the German offensive with optimism and relief. The newspapers of Saturday 11th May reflected and encouraged the popular mood with complacent comments on the situation. But even while Frenchmen read the comfortable phrases, the first streams of refugees, from Belgium and Luxembourg, were flowing across the French frontiers. Soon, to belie the false confidence being fostered by Press and Government through the agency of the Ministry of Information, the streams would reach flood proportions as the northern populations fled in droves from the Germans whose lightning advance nobody had anticipated or foretold.

That morning, with the aid of a large map in Reynaud's office in the Quai d'Orsay, a senior French liaison officer was explaining the position to Reynaud and some colleagues. The officer was worried at the ease with which the Allies were moving into Belgium and wondered if they were entering a trap. Reynaud, still concerned about the soundness of Plan D, telephoned his doubts to Daladier,

War Minister. 'Gamelin is in command', retorted Daladier, always Gamelin's staunch supporter, 'and he is putting his plans into execution.'

But on Day 2 the battle in the north looked less than promising. The Dutch were in retreat along with the French Seventh Army in Holland; and Holland's cities were being savagely air-attacked. The small Dutch air force had been immobilized and in the rear confusion was being spread by Dutch fifth columnists. The Belgians were faring little better. On the Albert Canal they began to abandon their positions to avoid being outflanked by a Panzer division of the XVI Armoured Corps which was crossing the undestroyed Maas bridges at Maastricht. At Liège, disastrously, the beleaguered fort of Eben-Emael fell, strengthening the enemy grip on the junction of the Meuse and the canal. But the worst ordeal came from the air, where the deadly German Stukas operated in a sky empty of Allied planes. They circled, dived and bombed with complete immunity, the new weapon that spread terror among troops who had no means of

resisting it, and among civilians whose only recourse seemed to be to herd onto the roads to try to escape from it.

The early Belgian setbacks were creating a problem for the French commander, General Prioux. In view of these and the undefended state of his Gembloux Gap sector, he was now concerned that his corps might be able to continue holding for long without support. He even doubted the efficacy of Plan D as it involved the French First Army. He signalled his views to General Georges, who undertook to expedite the First Army's arrival thus relieving his corps. At 8 pm on the 11th Prioux received a visit from the 1st Army Group commander, General Billotte, an old friend. Billotte stressed how vital it was for Prioux' troops to hold out. 'I have confidence in the Cavalry Corps,' he said. In the next three days that trust was going to be needed. Prioux' Cavalry Corps was to withstand a full-scale Panzer assault from the German XVI Armoured Corps as it crashed its way towards the Gembloux Gap.

With the Belgian Army pulling back during the night of the 11th-12th to its Dyle line north of Louvain, Prioux' two divisions, whose combined armoured strength equalled only about two-thirds of that of one Panzer division, were left as the sole bar to the next advance by the Panzers that had stormed the Albert Canal-Meuse defences. Battle was joined the next afternoon (12th), as German tanks rumbled forward after a heavy Stuka raid to probe the centre of the French line at Hannut. Ending inconclusively that night, fighting resumed on the 13th. That afternoon, after bitter resistance, the French were forced back to the 'Perwez-Marchevolette Line' – the ten-mile wide anti-tank obstacle less than nine miles in front of the French First Army's Wavre-Namur positions. Next morning (14th), in a renewed assault, the Germans pierced the line but failed to get through in strength. Meanwhile, the First Army formations had been moving into place, enabled to do so by Prioux' stalwart delaying action.

So, by that evening, the Plan D line

between Antwerp and Namur was established. Three Allied armies – the Belgians between Antwerp and Louvain, the BEF on the Dyle between Louvain and Wavre, the French First Army between Wavre and Namur – were in place across the centre of Belgium. But events had not gone entirely according to schedule. Summing-up on the 12th after three days of fighting, a Vincennes staff officer, Colonel Minart, had particularly noted the Belgians' inability to hold the Albert Canal line, and German dominance in the air. He also commented on the inadequacy of the information reaching Supreme Headquarters. This, of course, was a facet of the unwieldy command structure, whose drawbacks were already becoming apparent. With the three main headquarters (Vincennes,

Below: A German anti-tank company advances through the Ardennes
Right: The German tank break-through

Montry, La Ferté) separated by up to thirty miles, liaison was proving difficult. Between them there was a constant traffic of staff cars as Gamelin and Doumenc visited Georges and each other, sometimes twice a day. Moreover, Montry's lack of tele-printers necessitated an hourly dispatch-rider service to Vincennes with Intelligence reports.

La Ferté itself, the main operational HQ, scattered and rambling, was eminently unsuited to its purpose. Equally so was Georges' own command post, Les Bondons, a small country villa some miles off. Here the C-in-C occupied one of four ground-floor rooms, with little privacy and surrounded by the continuous clatter and bustle of busy clerks, orderlies and officers. And for General Claudel Georges, compactly built, bronzed from long overseas service, and rated one of France's ablest generals, there was an added handicap. In October 1934, accompanying King Alexander

of Jugoslavia through Marseilles, he had been gravely wounded by the killer who had assassinated that ill-fated monarch, and his health had been permanently impaired. But in his heavy burden of command he was greatly helped by General Doumenc who, lean, agile and forceful, daily spent long hours in conference with him at Les Bondons.

If the 14th May saw the Dyle Plan in operation, it produced a not unexpected reverse. Late that day the small Dutch Army, after five days' battle against overwhelming odds, surrendered. For the Allies the immediate effect of this was that Küchler's Eighteenth Army was released for action elsewhere. It also meant that the French Seventh Army, which had met severe resistance in executing its mission and whose main body had on the 14th been forced back across the Belgian border, could be withdrawn for other employment.

But for General Gamelin and the French High Command, new problems were now looming. In the last twenty-four hours it had been increasingly plain that the real German offensive was being staged not in central Belgium but on the neglected sector of the Franco-Belgian Meuse front between Namur and Sedan.

The stage was already being set on Day 2 of the offensive. As the 11th had dawned over the Ardennes nothing stood between the advancing German Panzer columns and the way into France and southern Belgium but the frail screen of Huntziger's and Corap's cavalry, and, behind these, a few ill-prepared French reserve divisions. By that evening, after further clashes in the southern clearings of the forest, the French patrol units had been decisively repulsed by elements of Guderian's XIX Armoured Corps, and the 1st Panzer Division had reached the outskirts of Bouillon, within ten miles of Sedan, across the Meuse in France. Twenty-four hours later

Above: German assault troops cross the Meuse. *Left:* German storm troopers

Bouillon had fallen, 1st Panzers had crossed the French frontier north of Sedan, and the cavalry of both the Ninth and Second Armies was back on the left bank of the Meuse, leaving the road open for the massed array of approaching armour, whose advance guard stood, as dusk fell, within a stone's throw of the vital river-line.

Meanwhile, forty miles north, another German breakthrough threatened the Belgian Meuse. Roughly parallel with Guderian's corps, General Hoth's Panzer corps – the northern prong of the three-pointed armoured spearhead, had been forging towards Dinant; and on the afternoon of 12th May leading units of the 7th Armoured Division, commanded by the dashing and dynamic Erwin Rommel, raced

forward to within a few miles of Houx, just north of Dinant. So, by the end of Day 3, the Germans had reached the Meuse at both ends of the Second and Ninth Army sectors.

For the French the three-day Ardennes operation had proved a costly failure. They had suffered heavy losses without appreciably delaying or inconveniencing the enemy Panzers. But before being thrown back across the river they had at least succeeded in blowing all the bridges over the Meuse and its tributary, the Chiers. (Thorough preparations had been made for this by both Huntziger and Corap, and accusations to be made soon after by Paul Reynaud – to explain away the Meuse disaster – that some bridges had been left undestroyed, were incontrovertibly refuted by official evidence.) That evening of 12th May two signals went from General Georges' La Ferté headquarters to Supreme Headquarters. One reported the mining of all Meuse and Chiers bridges except for those which would be blown after the last troops had crossed. The other stated tersely: 'The defence now seems well assured on the whole Meuse front.'

The section of the Meuse (the great river, some 560 miles long, which flows from Langres, in France's Haute-Marne, through Belgium and Holland, where it becomes the Maas and splits into two branches) assigned to the French Army in May 1940 ran from a point east of Sedan to Namur, in Belgium – about ninety miles in all. Though called by the French a 'sleepy' river, almost every place on this placid, winding stretch of the Meuse recalls past battles between French and Germans, in the First World War or earlier. Sedan, a small clothworking and garrison town at the foot of the wooded hills which rise beyond the right bank of the Meuse, had notably been a battleground both in 1870 when it was the scene of a historic French defeat, and again in 1914 when it quickly fell to the Germans. To the west and north, other Meuse positions fell equally quickly in 1914: ancient Mézières with its citadel; the small industrial town of Givet; cliff-dominated Dinant; Namur, ringed by its powerful forts. In the easy German storming of the Meuse on this occasion lay a warning for the French which, judging by later events, was less than fully appreciated.

The Meuse varies markedly between Sedan and Namur. In the Sedan area, where it is some sixty yards wide, it is more open than farther northwestwards towards the Belgian frontier. On each side the hills slope fairly gently down to river-level, giving a good field of fire to the opposite bank. These features characterized the Second Army's sector, Sedan-Mézières; but the Meuse in the Ninth Army's sector, Mézières-Namur, was very different. Northward from Mézières to Givet the Meuse valley quickly becomes narrower, deeper and more winding, with wooded banks and rocky cliffs dropping steeply to the river's edge. From Givet to Namur the river occasionally widens but remains mostly enclosed. But, to be effective, the natural defences of the whole Sedan-Namur stretch needed strong reinforcement. A test of Sedan's defences in 1938 had shown the town to be specially vulnerable to attack, but though defence works for it had been planned, up to December 1939 little had been done. Then, in March 1940, two French MPs (Deputies) had inspected the Meuse defences of both the Second and Ninth Armies and reported highly adversely on them. But still little action was taken. When the May offensive broke, preparations remained woefully defective, with casemates and other works uncompleted.

And what of the troops who were to man these Meuse defences, the soldiers of the French Ninth and Second Armies? The Ninth Army, composed of Bretons, Normans, men of the Loire, contained the highest quota of older reservists and static troops of any army stationed outside the Maginot Line. Of its seven infantry divisions, four were reservist, of which two – the 53rd and 61st Infantry – were 'Series B', classed by the war historian Theodore Draper as 'definitely inferior, badly armed, overaged and under-trained'. Another, the 102nd Infantry, was a fixed-defence fortress formation. This was unrewarding material to work on: indeed, for 62-year-old General André-Georges

German Stukas sowed panic and disruption in front of the advancing German ground troops

Corap, short, stoutish and reserved in manner, command of the Ninth Army was a thankless task, for the Ninth seemed dogged by neglect from the start. It was starved of weapons, including field artillery, anti-tank and anti-aircraft guns and tanks, of which last a third of its complement of 200 were last-war types. Right up to 10th May the deficiencies persisted, despite Corap's repeated demands to GHQ. It was small wonder that the men were wanting in morale and discipline as they soldiered half-heartedly through the months of the 'phoney war'. Small

wonder, too, that when the clash finally came, they were totally unprepared.

Huntziger's Second Army was in similar state as regards training, discipline, equipment and personnel. Predominantly a reservist army, it had two 'Series B' divisions, the 55th and 71st, as mediocre as Corap's 53rd and 61st, but with an equally vital defensive role. The men of the 55th hailed largely from the Bourges area and Loire Valley. With an average age of over thirty they were the army's *'crocos'*, 'old soldiers' who had for-

gotten much of what they had learned in their one-year service. Of its 450 officers, too, all but twenty were reservist. The 71st, made up of Parisians, was little different. Yet while a certain lethargy prevailed at General Corap's HQ at Vervins, at General Huntziger's HQ in the wooded Argonne village of Senuc the tone, set by Huntziger himself, was brisk and austere. Slim, erect and distinguished-looking, the general was admired for his sharp mind and infallible memory. Sensitive to his army's shortcomings, he did his best to remedy them, even trying to boost morale with a fortnightly news-sheet. But this was soon killed by apathy. Nevertheless, as late as mid-April 1940 Huntziger himself seemed strangely confident about the defendability of the Meuse line. He told the Controller-General of the Army that the Germans would not attack. 'On the contrary,' he added, 'they are frightened that we are going to do so.'

Among the French High Command all illusions about the Germans' real intentions had vanished on the 13th May. That morning, in General Doumenc's office at GHQ, Montry, the staff officer Captain Beaufre, studying the war map, clearly perceived that the main enemy effort was no longer in Belgium above Liège, but along an axis Luxembourg-Mézières. With a charcoal crayon he quickly sketched in the new line for colleagues to see. The same conclusion was being reached at Supreme Headquarters, Vincennes, where the calm optimism felt on Day 1 was beginning to wane. Gamelin's new-found misgivings were expressed in an order he issued at 1am on the 13th: 'We must now stand up to the onslaught of the enemy's mechanized and motorized forces. The hour has come to fight all-out on the positions fixed by the High Command. We no longer have any right to retreat.' The bleak injunction contrasted oddly with the buoyant call of three days before: 'We shall get them!'

As French GHQ painfully awoke to reality, the German commanders were actually planning to storm the Meuse. Late on the 12th Kleist had ordered Guderian to be ready to launch his XIX Armoured Corps across the river at 4pm on the 13th. At his Bouillon headquarters Guderian drew up his assault-plan: with Sedan as the centre of attack, advance units of the 2nd, 1st and 10th Panzer Divisions, deployed from west to east, were to cross the Meuse in a close, three-pronged thrust against the French Second Army positions. The Germans were setting themselves an easier task than they had a right to expect, for by the end of the 12th Huntziger's key troops were still, owing to a belated shuffle of divisions, not at their battle stations. The vital formation, defending the Sedan area, was General Grandsard's X Corps; and into the middle of X Corps, comprising General Lafontaine's 55th Infantry Division on the left and General Chapouilly's 3rd North African Division on the right, had at the last moment been inserted the 71st Division (General Baudet) from the rear. In consequence, at dawn on the 13th the divisions were still confusedly manoeuvring into their new places.

Ironically, east of Sedan on a sector not threatened, and abutting the Maginot Line, were two of Huntziger's best divisions (XVIII Corps, General Rochard): the 'active' 3rd Colonial and the 'Series A' reservist 41st. Moreover the Second Army's weakness in the Sedan sector itself was matched by the feebleness of its neighbour on the left, the Ninth Army. Here, across the vulnerable junction point of Corap's and Huntziger's armies – from Sedan to Mézières – the two generals had placed four of their poorest divisions. In one continuous line stood Corap's 61st Infantry and 102nd Garrison Divisions, and Huntziger's 55th and 71st Infantry Division – the 'crocos', the static fortress troops, the least battleworthy soldiers of two mediocre armies.

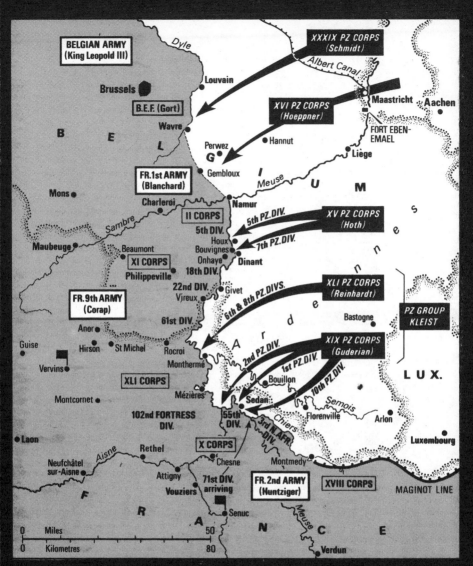

The Panzers strike westward

Marshalling against these unimpressive forces, in their flimsy, unfinished defences, were the leading elements of five armoured divisions – Guderian's 2nd, 1st and 10th opposite Sedan, and Reinhardt's 6th and 8th opposite Monthermé (shortly to the west), in the centre of General Libaud's XLI Corps (Ninth Army) sector. Away to the northwest, opposite the Ninth Army's XI Corps sector around Dinant on the Belgian Meuse, the 5th and 7th Panzers of Hoth's XV Armoured Corps were assembling. And behind the advanced armour and assault-troops, on this night of 12th-13th May, followed the miles-long mechanized columns, their unmasked lights shining through the forest. The great approach-move through the Ardennes, so meticulously planned, was going precisely as scheduled. In front of the weary officers and men halted on the river banks, and those still heading westwards to the Meuse, there now loomed the next and most crucial phase of the momentous operation – the breakthrough.

If Huntziger's Second Army divisions were still in some disarray, Corap's forces were likewise unready. On the northern flank, south of Namur, the 5th Motorized Division (General

Boucher) of General Bouffet's II Corps was in place, as were the 61st Infantry Division (General Vauthier) and 102nd Garrison Division (General Portzert) of Libaud's XLI Corps, which manned the Ninth Army's southeastern-most sector from Vireux, south of Givet, to Pont-à-Bar; but the coverage of the central sector, from Dinant to Vireux, remained perilously sparse. This was allocated to General Martin's XI Corps; but by the end of the 12th only a sprinkling of these reservists (18th Infantry Division, General Duffet, and 22nd Infantry Division, General Hassler) had arrived.

The 18th Infantry's piece-meal arrival was unfortunate, for it was just north of Dinant, at Houx, where advance units of Rommel's 7th Armoured Division had reached that afternoon; and it was here that, during the night of 12th-13th, an enemy motorcycle patrol crossed the river and later stormed the heights to break up a newly-installed unit of the 18th Infantry. Despite intervention by the neighbouring 5th Motorized Division, the Germans pressed on inland. Meanwhile, at 10am on the 13th, they made another crossing at Bouvignes, south of Houx. By noon, swarming across on boats, rafts, canoes and even by swimming, the enemy had established a bridgehead around Houx two miles deep and three wide.

This news sent a shock of alarm through all the rear headquarters. Urgent orders to counterattack came from General Martin at corps, General Billotte at army group, and General Georges himself. But for various unsatisfactory reasons no counterattack materialised. Night fell with Rommel's men firmly lodged on the heights above the Meuse's left bank. And meanwhile the Ninth Army was facing another crisis. On the 13th its front was being pierced in a second place: forty miles south, around hill-flanked Monthermé, where the Meuse met the twisting river Semois, General Portzert's 102nd Garrison Division was being violently attacked by advance units of XLI Armoured Corps – the centre spike of the great three-headed thrust launched against the Meuse that day.

After enemy movements had been spotted across the river opposite Monthermé, in itself a surprise for the almost totally unprepared 102nd, the assault started at 3pm. Two battalions of the 6th Panzers, breaking the fierce initial resistance from the 102nd's strong-points (such as they were) and artillery, stormed over the river. Supported by tank-gun fire from the right bank the Germans gained the heights beyond Monthermé, and later more troops followed on to strengthen the bridgehead. By nightfall Reinhardt's men, digging in before the French second defence line, had virtually isolated the vulnerable Givet Peninsula, the tongue of French territory protruding into Belgium to their north. And to their south stretched the virtually undefended lands of France.

Meanwhile, thirty miles southeast of Monthermé, a fiercer battle had been raging. Guderian's advance units had struck a heavy blow at Sedan, preceded by a massive and pulverising bombing attack. For six hours the X Corps reservists had cowered under the bombs of the Stukas which, more effectively than any gunfire, were to prepare the way for the Sedan landings. The onslaught had fallen on the luckless 55th and 71st Divisions, who least of all were trained or equipped to withstand such *Blitzkrieg* tactics and were still barely settled in their new positions. The bombers, from General Sperrle's Third Air Force, had been called in by Guderian, whose artillery had not yet arrived. Mostly Stukas, they began coming over about 9am, intensifying their attack two hours later and continuing until mid-afternoon. No less than twelve dive-bomber squadrons operated over Sedan that day, with precise orders from Guderian to obliterate the French defences. This they most effectively did, speedily silencing whatever coun-

terfire the French managed to put up, and reducing the forward defence lines to a shambles. But most telling was the bombers' effect on the troops, who were totally demoralised by the sustained assault of these plummeting aircraft with their screaming bombs, the more so as no opposing Allied plane appeared in the skies that day. An appeal from General Lafontaine to Second Army HQ for air support was unproductive.

At 2pm General Gransard, X Corps commander, ordered forward two reserve infantry regiments and a reserve tank battalion to a prepared line south of Sedan. Two hours later, against a shattered and virtually immobilised defence, Guderian launched his ground attack. The 1st Panzer assault troops – elements of a motorcycle battalion, a lorried infantry brigade and the crack Gross Deutschland infantry regiment – gained the left bank near Gaulier, west of Sedan. With little difficulty they achieved their immediate objective, the cap-

ture of the small river loop forming the Iges Peninsula, including Glaire and Torcy; and almost unopposed by the stunned, smoke-blinded French they raced on towards Frenois, Marfée Wood and other inland points, cutting off Sedan from behind.

Simultaneously the 10th Panzer assault force landed near Wadelincourt, just southeast of Sedan – though not so easily. Caught by flanking fire from undestroyed strongpoints, they found themselves pinned in a narrow zone round Wadelincourt. West of Sedan the 2nd Panzer Division, not yet fully deployed, failed to put over any troops. But these setbacks were outweighed by the swift success of the 1st Panzers, who by sunset had breached the French defence line at the base of Marfée Wood, two miles south of Sedan. As the day ended there was a German bridgehead around the town, four miles wide and four deep.

So on the 13th the Germans had gained, at Houx, Monthermé and Sedan, three footholds across the Meuse. But at this early stage there was nothing irreparable about these gains. Only small forces were involved, with no tanks or heavy guns. In all three places the enemy was vulnerable to a determined counter-blow. Huntziger, visiting X Corps headquarters around 6pm, saw the Sedan position as still within control and ordered Grandsard to plug the gap and then counterattack. At GHQ, La Ferté, General Georges himself was not unduly worried by the situation. Reporting to Supreme Headquarters, Vincennes, on the enemy progress, he added: 'the air bombing is continuous, but is not harming the troops.' This may well have been true as regards casualties; but it was probably owing to the devastating effect of the relentless six-hour strafe on their morale that, soon after, these unseasoned X Corps units gave way to a wild and widespread panic.

**German storm troops in action . . .
their equipment was superior**

Collapse at Sedan

The immediate cause of the panic was a rumour that flashed through the 55th Division's sector about 6pm that enemy tanks were across the Meuse. One such story emanated from a X Corps battery commander at Chaumont (east of Marfée Wood), who spotted 'departure lights' near Marfée Wood and immediately reported the suspected presence of enemy tanks to the corps artillery command post at Flaba. Then another unit reported more tanks moving south from the Wadelincourt area. Within minutes, men were running from their posts with cries of 'Enemy tanks'. Others joined them as they retreated, and soon the roads from Sedan were crowded with troops, horses and vehicles heading out of the battle zone.

In fact, no German tanks crossed the Meuse on 13th May. The Sedan defenders were being panicked by a few of their own tanks, moving in support towards nearby Bulson. Those who had not seen 'enemy' tanks blindly believed those who declared they had. One French commander, General Ruby, called it a 'phenomenon of collective hallucination'. The situation was worsened by the wrecking of communications caused by the prolonged bombing: command posts were isolated, formation headquarters were left unaware of what was happening in the forward areas and unable to exercise any control. Once started the mass hysteria was not only unstoppable but was so quickly infectious that it permeated divisional and even corps headquarters.

The panic gathered force as it reached the rear. At his command post at Fond-Dagot, General Lafontaine (55th Division) was surprised around 6pm by a crowd of soldiers from two infantry and two artillery regiments fleeing southwards and shouting that the tanks were at Bulson. With his staff he dashed into the road in an effort to stop them. Elsewhere officers were joining in the rout, claiming that they had been ordered to retire. Their example incited more troops to quit. As the rearward artillery command posts emptied, forward gunners – still manning their guns against the advancing Germans but now without fire orders –

found themselves stranded, and they decamped too. The hysteria was striking deepest among the corps and divisional heavy artillery. At Bulson an artillery group commander reported to his superior nearby that there was fighting 500 yards from Bulson and that he was about to be encircled by enemy machine-gunners and asked leave to withdraw. This was granted, and both commanders ordered their entire groups to retire and abandoned their command posts.

General Lafontaine himself was involved in the flight. Without waiting to check a report of an imminent German advance, his staff obtained General Grandsard's permission to move the 55th's command post south to Chémery. By car and afoot the staff headed precipitately out of Fond-Dagot, leaving a deserted headquarters. Smoke rose into the evening air from hurriedly burned files. Lafontaine's party reached Chémery amid pandemonium, as fleeing troops and transport columns surged through the village. Along with X Corps gunners, much of the 55th Division seemed on the move. In these circumstances

Lafontaine now, on General Grandsard's orders, had the almost impossible task of organising a counterattack by all available X Corps reserves, for dawn next day. Towards midnight he sent out three officers to different points to check and report back on the whereabouts of his units, but with such discouraging results that he decided it was impossible to proceed with the counterattack without further briefing from Grandsard. However, driving to X Corps headquarters at La Berlière, he found the roads so choked that he was forced to turn back without seeing him.

From the 55th Division, the disarray had quickly spread to the 71st. General Baudet's divisional command post at Raucourt was thrown into a flurry by a telephone report allegedly coming from X Corps Chief of Staff, Colonel Badel, that enemy tanks had reached Chaumont. Badel directed Baudet to form a defensive loop and move up infantry and tanks to prepare a counterattack. Minutes later Badel called again, reporting that the enemy tanks were at Bulson and General Lafontaine was evacuating his command post. Thereupon General Baudet decided to leave his own headquarters, and with his divisional artillery commander drove off to La Bagnolle, on the western edge of the 71st's sector. As with the 55th Division, the abandonment of senior artillery command posts added to the débâcle. Distraught gunners strove vainly to contact rear headquarters staffs which had already made off. But against the great stream of retreat, some units stood fast and even pressed forward under the leadership of cool and intrepid officers like the artilleryman, Captain Benedetti, and the infantry commander, Lieutenant-Colonel Montvignier-Monnet.

For a few crucial hours the disorderly retreat of the Sedan troops was threatening to immobilise the whole sector. As well as halting vital traffic to the front, it was impeding the transmission of orders and information. And some orders that seemingly did get through had a mysterious aspect. In several cases retirement instructions appear to have been given by individuals purporting to be officers but who were unknown to the troops. There were also instances of unidentified telephone orders that seemed deliberately aimed at increasing the confusion. In the rear, moreover, allegedly bogus orders drew civilians into the rout. Was all this the work of enemy agents, who might have infiltrated across the frontier in the guise of fugitives?

That night the panic spread to Second Army units thirty miles south of Sedan. To control the growing flood of runaways, the Second Army Provost Marshal called in extra *gardes mobiles*. Echoes of the stampede even reached Second Army headquarters with the arrival at Senuc of two excited officers asking to see General Huntziger. They told the general they had seen German tanks at Vendresse, ten miles south of Sedan. Scathingly Huntziger retorted that what they had taken to be German Panzers was the Second Army's 7th Tank Battalion.

At Supreme Headquarters this had been a day of shocks. The successive reports of the Meuse crossings had caused growing concern in the dank underground offices. Gamelin and his staff had now to accept that the whole strategic picture had changed for the worse. It was clear that the German moves south of Namur could, unless checked, threaten the success of Plan D. But the only hint of the Sedan dèbâcle received that day was an evening signal from Georges at La Ferté, reporting 'quite serious trouble' south of Sedan and adding that the 3rd Armoured Division had been called. But from a later signal to Vincennes (received at 11.45pm) it seemed that Georges himself was at this stage unaware of the Second Army's collapse. 'We are calm – *nous sommes calmes,*' reassuringly ran this message.

At GHQ, Montry, likewise, there was on the 13th no knowledge of the Sedan trouble. But about 2am on the 14th Captain Beaufre was roused at Montry by a telephone call from General Georges. 'Ask General Doumenc to come immediately,' Beaufre was directed. By 3am Doumenc, along with Beaufre, arrived at Les Bondons – to witness an extraordinary scene. As graphically described by Beaufre, the room was in semi-darkness and the atmosphere funereal. There was silence except for the quiet voice of a staff officer on the telephone. General Roton, Georges' Chief of Staff, was slumped despondently in a chair. As they entered, Georges, looking pale, walked up to Doumenc. 'Our Sedan front is broken!' he cried. 'There's been a collapse.' He sat down, stifling a sob.

As Doumenc listened astounded, Georges explained that the 55th and 71st Divisions had 'given ground' after severe bombing: that X Corps HQ had reported that the line was broken and enemy tanks had reached Bulson about midnight. He gave vent to more

**British Blenheims depart
on reconnoitring mission to Germany**

44

sobs. Breaking the embarrassed silence, Doumenc said briskly: 'Come, general. Every war has seen its routs. Come over to the map. We'll see what can be done.' Pointing at the big wallchart, he roughed out a plan involving the three French armoured divisions, hitherto in reserve. The 1st, in Belgium and detailed to take part in the Dyle operation, could counterattack from north to south on Corap's front; the 3rd, just south of Sedan, could attack from south to north. The 2nd Armoured Division, *en route* northwards to the Dyle, could be detrained at Vervins and deployed for a west-east attack. These three divisions, urged Doumenc, comprising 600 tanks, could assault the enemy concentrically and throw him back over the Meuse. The 3rd, at Sedan, could engage next morning, he added. Doumenc's confident-sounding scheme eased the tension and Georges quickly confirmed all the proposals and issued appropriate orders. Beaufre rang for the mess cook to make coffee, and soon afterwards he and Doumenc left, somewhat relieved, for Montry.

But, if Doumenc had given Georges new hope that night, the grim fact remained that everything – and this included the survival of the Allied armies in Belgium – depended on the French ability to launch effective counter blows at Houx, Monthermé and Sedan with the least possible delay.

As this was being uneasily recognized by the French High Command on Tuesday 14th May, Germany's military chiefs at OKW (High Command of the Armed Forces) and OKH (High Command of the Army) were assessing the position with great satisfaction. Except that the Dutch were resisting longer than expected, Plan Yellow was proceeding entirely according to schedule. The Allied armies were disposed just as Hitler had foreseen they would be when framing his Ardennes strategy, and his forces had gained footholds over the Meuse, as specified in the Führer's Directive No 10 of the previous February. Now, on Day 5 of the Battle of the West, he issued his Directive No 11, giving General von Rundstedt (Army Group A) *carte blanche* to develop his all-out advance from the Meuse to the Channel. The Directive's paragraph two stated:

'. . . the swift forcing of the Meuse crossing in the sector of Army Group A has established the first essentials for a thrust in all possible strength north of the Aisne and in a northwesterly direction, as laid down in Directive No 10. Such a thrust might produce a major success. It is the task of forces engaged north of the line Liège-Namur to deceive and hold down the greatest number of enemy forces by attacking them with their own resources.'

Against such 'a thrust in all possible strength' neither the Ninth nor the Second Army could now offer much resistance. Though the Ninth Army had suffered no major breakdown like the Second, Corap's troops were hardly capable of holding their existing line, let alone counterattack. The main body of General Martin's XI Corps (manning the central sector) had arrived only the previous day and found no prepared positions. Moreover, the advance units had made the initial mistake of digging-in on the heights above the Meuse instead of on the riverbanks. Now Martin's illtrained and ill-equipped reservists found themselves defending a section of unfamiliar front, one part of which was already pierced. And now, to them as to other Ninth Army formations, 14th May was to bring fresh setbacks. At dawn, in an effort to repel the invaders, two 5th Motorized Division units (II Corps, north of XI Corps) made an unsuccessful attack. Meanwhile, the Meuse line was being breached at two new points, north and south of Houx. At the latter point, the tanks of Rommel's 7th Panzer Division crossed the river at Bouvignes on German-built pontoons. Rommel now planned to dash straight on through the Philippeville 'Gap', twenty miles west. With his leading riflemen and

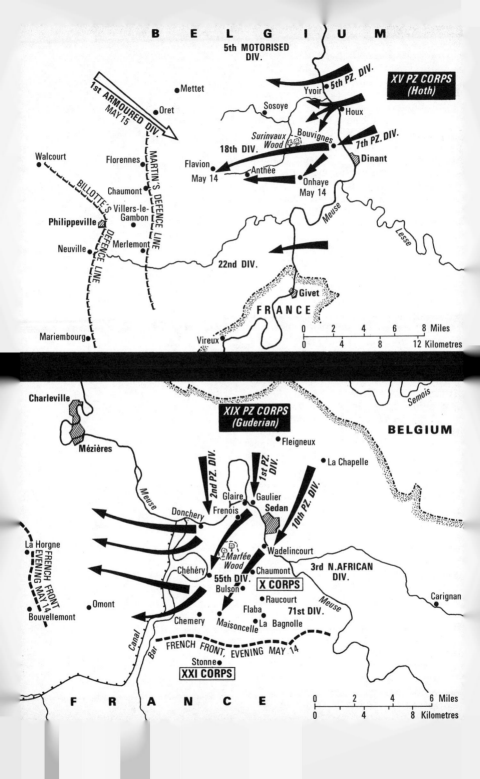

motorcyclists faced only by scattered elements of General Duffet's 18th Division, by midmorning he had taken Surinvaux, Hontoire, Flavion and other places.

He then attacked Onhaye, which barred the passage through the Philippeville Gap. Onhaye fell late that afternoon, and the 7th Panzers headed westwards against opposition from elements of the 18th Division, reserve 4th North African Division and 1st Light Cavalry Division. At the day's end little remained of the 18th's defence lines. And on the 18th's right, the 22nd Division was also in trouble. Partially over-run in the morning by Germans crossing the Meuse north of Givet, it had been ordered back to a position six miles from the river, and by evening was in contact with the Meuse only south of Vireux, and retreating in disorder. In an effort to save the situation, General Martin decided to redeploy XI Corps, along with the 4th North Africans, on a line linking it with XLI Corps on his right. But before this could be done, orders arrived for a general retirement of the Ninth Army.

General Corap had spent the morning moving between his formation headquarters, striving to avert the mounting disintegration. He noted with concern his troops' faltering morale – largely the result of the continuous air attacks. He was disturbed too at the poor bearing of some officers. That day he issued an order: '. . . At the moment when the fate of France is in jeopardy, no weakness will be tolerated. It is incumbent on staffs to give an example to all ranks and, if necessary, compel obedience. . .' But the wavering divisions of XI and XLI Corps were now no longer amenable to warnings: they were losing all cohesion as a fighting force. From Dinant to Monthermé, the centre of the Ninth Army's Meuse line, with the exception of the left flank of the 102nd

British Hurricanes, the mainstay of the RAF

Panzerkampfwagen Pzkpfw-111F
The standard medium tank of the German Panzer divisions at the time of the invasion of France. *Weight:* 20 tons. *Speed:* 24 mph. *Crew:* five. *Armour:* 30-mm. *Armament:* one 50-mm gun, two 7.92-mm machine-guns

Panzerkampfwagen Pzkpfw-11
The Pzkpfw-11 comprised the majority of the tanks of the German armoured regiments at the outbreak of war in 1939. It was essentially a lightly-armed scout tank. *Weight:* 10 tons. *Speed:* 30 mph. *Crew:* three. *Armour:* 15-mm (max). *Armament:* one 20-mm cannon, one 7.92-mm machine-gun

The Pzkw IVB
The best tank in service with German Panzer divisions, the Pzkw IVB, was unfortunately only available in limited numbers, but nevertheless did much valuable work. Although it had a gun as large as that in the Char B, its armour was only half as thick. Specification: *Weight:* 17.7 tons. *Armament:* one 75mm gun and two 7.9mm machine guns. *Crew:* 5 men. *Maximum speed:* 25 mph. *Armour:* 30mm maximum. *Engine:* 320 hp. *Length:* 19 feet 3 inches. *Width:* 9 feet 4¼ inches

The T-38 light tank
The T-38, a Czech design, was taken in large quantities after Munich, and served with the Panzer divisions as their best light tank, equipping most of Rommel's 7th Panzer Division. Specification: *Weight:* 11 tons. *Armament:* one 37mm gun and one 7.9mm machine gun. *Crew:* 4 men. *Maximum speed:* 35 mph. *Armour:* 50mm maximum. *Engine:* 125 hp. *Length:* 14 feet 11½ inches. *Width:* 6 feet 7¼ inches

Garrison Division which stood fast and held up Reinhardt's assault troops for two days, was crumbling.

This was a triumph for the German *blitzkrieg* tactics – a victory for surprise, violence, speed and mobility. And before being outpaced and outfought by the mechanized onslaught of Rommel's tanks, the French had been subjected to the low-level bombing attacks that had spread destruction and demoralization at front and rear. At various points their retirement became a rout. 'Panic gripped some troops in the course of withdrawal,' wrote General Doumenc, who noted the devastating effect of the bombing. In the Ninth Army's rear the roads were crowded with truckloads of troops mingled with swarms of fleeing civilians. In the woods other soldiers sought refuge from the ubiquitous planes and tanks.

By evening (the 14th) the bulk of three Ninth Army divisions were retreating from the Meuse in disorder, westwards through Belgian Namur and southwestwards into France's Aisne department. Many troops were angry and embittered, seeing themselves as victims of events beyond their control, fatally handicapped by inadequate equipment. They also blamed, as one man put it, 'the absence of French artillery and aircraft, the shock of the bombings, and the overwhelming flood of refugees.'

Yet during the 14th, the disaster might have been arrested by the rapid intervention, as General Doumenc had proposed to Georges the previous night, of the 1st Armoured Division (General Bruneau). But by a calamitous series of delays the division was prevented from reaching the front in these crucial hours. When alerted for action on the morning of the 14th it was at Charleroi, twenty miles back from the Meuse, but it was 1.30pm before General Bruneau was called to Martin's command post at Florennes for briefing, and 5pm when he actually arrived there. He was then directed to attack as soon as possible towards

Dinant. The division headed east from Charleroi in early evening, but was so hampered by crowded roads that only part reached its rendezvous that night – and the attack was postponed until next day.

Meanwhile another chapter of accidents was stopping the 3rd Armoured Division (General Brocard) from salvaging the Sedan front. By nightfall, with the Second Army's left-flank and and centre positions virtually nonexistent, the chance for an armoured counterblow had passed.

To replace the shattered X Corps, early on the 14th Huntziger had assigned the defence of the Sedan sector to General Flavigny's XXI Corps, comprising the 3rd Armoured, 3rd Mechanized and 5th Light Cavalry Divisions. Though the 3rd Armoured comprised two battalions of B tanks, two of H tanks, a towed-artillery regiment and lorry-borne infantry, its strength was mostly on paper, and, as later alleged by the division's Chief of Staff, General Devaux, it had begun training as a complete formation only on 1st May, and with various deficiencies was unready for combat, though the troops' morale was good.

The 3rd Armoured, along with the 3rd Mechanized Division, arrived at le Chesne, nine miles from the battle-zone, at about dawn on the 14th. Ahead of them lay the vista of hamlets

German infantry move through a wrecked French village

and wooded hills sloping to the Meuse, scene of yesterday's Sedan débâcle. Brocard planned to attack at noon in the Chémery-Maisoncelle direction, making a massed sortie from the north edge of Maison-Dieu Wood. But now the delays began: and it was 4pm when the division was finally deployed. Thirty minutes earlier, however, the operation had been called off: Flavigny, at his Senuc command post, had changed his mind and now ordered the 3rd to extend in defensive positions right across the Second Army zone from Omont to Stonne. The counterattack was postponed until next afternoon.

Brocard's later arrival, seemingly due to refuelling and slow passing of orders, had left the fully prepared 3rd Mechanized Division unsupported. Huntziger was furious to learn of the operation's postponement and ordered Flavigny to investigate the reasons personally. The sorry result of this failure was that, with Guderian's Panzers crossing the Meuse that day, at no time on the 14th were they confronted by the French 3rd Armoured Division. It fell to the improvised 55th Division force, hastily assembled by Lafontaine the previous evening, to face the German tanks.

But even this action was dogged by delays. The first group of Lafontaine's mixed tanks–and–infantry force,

ordered to advance by stages to the Meuse, moved off at 7am instead of at dawn, and ninety minutes later met a strong Panzer column between Chémery and Chéhéry. Badly battered, it retired to Maison-Dieu Wood. Lafontaine thereupon cancelled the second group's advance, thus ruling out the last chance of a counterattack by the 55th Division. The 55th's abdication signalled the breakup of the 71st Division, on its right. With its west flank exposed, the 71st pulled back eastwards, and this sudden withdrawal started another rout among the already demoralized troops. During the day the command increasingly lost its grip on the situation; and by nightfall the 71st had ceased to count as a fighting force.

Meanwhile, by noon that day the German Panzers were dominating the Sedan battlefield. The 1st and 2nd Armoured Divisions were across the Meuse in force and heading inland, and the 10th was still assembling along the left bank. Guderian was now anxious to drive on westward with all speed towards the Channel. That afternoon he ordered the 1st (General Veiel) and 2nd (General Kuchner) to wheel west, Veiel's division on a northerly line towards Flize and Sapogne, and Kuchner's on a southerly track towards Vendresse. Their southern flank he left guarded by the Gross Deutschland infantry division. The 10th would advance shortly from the Meuse, to veer westwards in its turn, with the 14th Motorized Division. But until it did, for a few crucial hours that afternoon there was a vulnerable gap in Guderian's armour – between the 1st and 2nd Divisions, rolling away westwards, and the 10th, marshalling on the river bank. Here lay a golden opportunity for intervention by Flavigny's XXI Corps – a chance that was thrown away through the 3rd Armoured Division's unreadiness.

The one resolute bid to counter the Sedan breakthrough on the 14th came from the air. For two waves of Allied bombers – French Potezes and Moranes, British Fairey Battles and Blenheims – blasted the advancing German columns and hastily-improvised bridges. But so intense was the flak that the bridges remained intact and over one hundred planes were lost. Yet even here there was a missed opportunity. Early that afternoon it was agreed by Lord Gort and Generals Gamelin and Georges that the British War Cabinet should be asked for the immediate use of the British home-based Bomber Force in the Sedan sector. But hopes were suddenly shattered when Georges announced that he would be satisfied with one hundred bombers only, from the French-based Bomber Command. 'All the dash and drive is left to the Germans,' lamented a British Intelligence officer.

Despite the gravity of the situation, at Second Army headquarters, Senuc, a strange optimism still prevailed. Visiting war correspondents were told that the Germans would be held on the army's main defence line. But reality intervened later that day when it was abruptly decided to withdraw headquarters to Verdun, thirty-five miles southeast. Arriving there that night, the tired Huntziger declared to one of his staff: 'I shall always

be the *vaincu* of Sedan.' As the Meuse front had crumbled, Huntziger had had little help from General Georges. Earlier he had urgently telephoned for guidance as to whether he should cover the Maginot Line or Paris. Georges had promised to call back but had not done so. When Huntziger had telephoned again the C-in-C had told him briefly: 'Do what seems best.'

General Georges was clearly being overwhelmed by the gigantic battle he was having to direct. His health, impaired ever since his Marseilles wounding in 1934, now showed signs of breaking. General Gamelin, visiting him at Les Bondons that day, was concerned at his appearance. Georges 'seemed truly exhausted', he noted. But even at that moment Georges seemed to be taking on himself further responsibility: for on the 14th he removed the Second Army from Billotte's 1st Army Group and placed it directly under his own command. And now, while Corap and Huntziger strove desperately but vainly, by throwing in such unemployed forces as they could muster, to hold the vulnerable Bar River line (junction line of the Ninth and Second Armies), Georges made a desperate effort to plug the widening gap that was ballooning out from the Meuse. From 200 miles away, in Eastern France, he summoned General Touchon, commanding the reserve Sixth Army.

But for the rest of that day Touchon, who only arrived at his command post at Rethel on the Aisne at 7pm, could do nothing. Only one new formation was available for blocking the gap on the 14th: General de Lattre de Tassigny's 14th Division, seconded from the distant Army of Alsace (General Bourret's Fifth Army), was hurrying north from the Rheims area. At Ninth Army HQ, Vervins, Corap ordered Tassigny to link with his (Corap's) reserve 53rd Division on the Ninth right, and there re-establish

The end for a British Fairey Battle

liaison with the Second Army. Tassigny led forward his small force (the bulk had not arrived) through fleeing Ninth Army men, only to find the 53rd Division had disappeared. Reporting back to Corap he was directed to hold the second defence position. But on arrival there he discovered the Germans had anticipated him.

Such was the picture of chaos and calamity on the Meuse front on 14th May. In Paris, the Government was following events here and in central Belgium with growing alarm. On learning, early that afternoon, of the Army's collapse, Reynaud asked whether the armies in Belgium had been ordered to withdraw. His chief liaison officer, telephoning Vincennes, found that they had not. 'We felt that the situation had suddenly become tragic,' commented Paul Baudouin, Secretary to the Cabinet. At 3pm the War Committee (normally comprising certain Ministers, the Supreme Commander, the Admiral of the Fleet and, as President, the President of the Republic) met to consider the position. Immediately afterwards Reynaud telephoned to Winston Churchill (British Prime Minister since 10th May) the following Government 'statement':

'The situation is indeed very serious. Germany is trying to deal us a fatal blow in the direction of Paris. The German Army has broken through our fortified lines south of Sedan . . . To stop the German drive . . . the German tanks must be isolated from their supporting Stukas. This is only possible through a considerable force of fighter aircraft . . . To win this battle . . . It is essential that you send immediately ten additional squadrons . . . I have confidence that, at this critical hour, British aid will not fail us.'

That evening, in Winston Churchill's Admiralty office in London, the British War Cabinet gravely considered Reynaud's somewhat alarming communication. At 8.30pm Churchill sent the following understandably non-committal reply: ' . . . We have called in Staff Officers who are in a position to give us details of the last-minute state of affairs, so that we can be sure that all available resources are employed to the utmost in the common cause.'

Failure of French armour

The small, dapper French Premier was little comforted by Winston Churchill's reply. After an anxious night he telephoned Churchill again at 7.30 next morning, repeating his plea for fighter aid and adding melodramatically: 'We are beaten. We have lost the battle.' Churchill, somewhat sceptical, tried to reassure him. 'But all is changed,' cried Reynaud agitatedly. 'A torrent of tanks is bursting through!' Churchill then telephoned General Georges and received a more encouraging report. The Sedan breach, said Georges, was being plugged. The suspicion that Reynaud was exaggerating seemed borne out by a telegram to Churchill from General Gamelin, stating that though the Namur-Sedan position was grave, Gamelin viewed the situation calmly. But in fact Reynaud's assessment was nearer the truth. On this morning of 15th May, as the Meuse line collapsed beyond recovery and the German armoured spearheads drove into Northern France, not only was France herself in danger, but a direct threat menaced Paris.

Gamelin took the Paris danger seriously enough to summon the capital's Military Governor, General Hering, and the Chief of Staff at the War Ministry, General Colson, to discuss emergency defence and evacuation measures. But in the bright May sunshine of that morning, Parisians went about their affairs ignorant of the looming danger, or even of the Meuse breakthrough. The Press, restricted to euphemisms, half-truths and optimistic speculation, was at the mercy of the official censorship which rigorously controlled the publication of war news. Broadcasting on the 13th, the Minister of Information had complacently remarked that Verdun and the Somme (First World War battles) had lasted six months. But the endurance that marked those campaigns was signally lacking along much of the present battlefront.

On the 15th the only sector of the Allied front where the armies were holding was in the centre. The BEF, its spirit high, was standing fast on the Louvain-Wavre line. To its right

the French First Army was stoutly
resisting the violent tank and infantry
onslaught of Reichenau's forces, and
the Stukas – unopposed by Allied
planes – of Kesselring's and Sperrle's
Air Forces. But while Lord Gort's and
General Blanchard's troops held firm,
in the north the Dutch Army had lain
down its arms, and in the south
Corap's and Huntziger's armies were
themselves facing defeat.

Through the night of the 14th/15th
the Ninth Army's retreat was being
hampered by conflicting orders. There
was confusion as to which of three
different defence lines – as prescribed
by Generals Billotte, Corap and
Martin – the retiring troops should
occupy; and as the bewildered units
blundered about in the dark, some
made for one line, some for another.
Some XI Corps troops even landed
back in France. This was sympto-
matic of the Ninth's steady disintegration. Its one formation still in position
was the 5th Motorized Division (II
Corps) on the extreme left. In the
centre Martin's XI Corps was fading
away southwestwards, the divisional

commanders hardly knowing where
their men were. South of XI Corps,
the two XLI Corps divisions, the 61st
Infantry and 102nd Garrison Divisions,
were likewise giving way under crush-
ing pressure.

At First Army Group headquarters,
General Billotte had become increasingly dissatisfied with Corap's
handling of the battle. He had in fact
decided that Corap was no longer
equal to his task and must be replaced. At 4am he had reported thus
to Georges, proposing that the Ninth
be taken over by General Giraud, the
Seventh Army's commander, who
now, with the surrender of the Dutch,
was available elsewhere. Georges
agreed, and Giraud, known as a bold
and vigorous general, was ordered to
report from Antwerp to Vervins that
afternoon. Corap was to take over the
Seventh Army.

Not only conflicting orders had been
hindering the retreat of the Ninth.
Its movements were being obstructed
by thousands of fleeing civilians, who
cumbered every road out of the battle
zone. At a moment's notice people

Left: General Giraud, Commander, French Seventh Army. *Above:* General Charles de Gaulle

were abandoning their homes in panic, seizing whatever possessions they could. Joining other refugees, they herded along the southbound routes in heavy-laden cars and carts, on horseback or on foot, carrying and wheeling their belongings, babies in the arms of mothers, old folk hobbling on sticks. 'A whole province is emptying,' wrote one observer. To the southeast, the same traffic was surging back behind the Second Army front. At Vouziers-sur-Aisne, twenty-five miles from Sedan, where refugees had thronged the streets all night, the hospital was full of civilians who had been wounded by low-level enemy planes while on the roads. It seemed that everywhere these sore-tried people were suffering from lack of direction and guidance, and they would in many cases have done better to stay where they were rather than take flight.

Meanwhile Guderian's leading Panzer units were heading away from the Meuse in a widening southwestward sweep. During the night of the 14th/15th they had advanced into the Ninth Army sector, but much of 10th Armoured Division was still in Second Army terrain, with its command post at Bulson. Available to oppose it was General Flavigny's yet uncommitted XXI Corps. Georges had ordered Huntziger to remount the attack by dispatching Brocard's 3rd Armoured Division towards the Meuse, and at dawn on the 15th Huntziger passed instructions to Flavigny for a strong tank-based operation. But at midmorning Flavigny amended the plan by ordering a mixed tanks-and-infantry action, putting the infantryman General Bertin-Boussu, commanding the 3rd Motorized Division, in command. By further modifications he diluted the scheme to a cautious, semi-defensive operation, with Brocard's tanks strung out among the infantry. Zero hour was 3pm, but as

Brocard could not re-deploy his tanks by then, it was changed to 5.30. But at that hour Brocard's tanks were still not ready; so Flavigny cancelled the attack.

Once more Flavigny's armour had failed to engage. But on the Namur front General Bruneau's 1st Armoured Division, summoned on the 14th to aid the wavering XI Corps, was in the midst of a bitter day-long struggle with Rommel's Panzers. Towards evening, with crippling tank losses, Bruneau ordered a general withdrawal to Beaumont, fifteen miles west of Philippeville. But, cut off by the fast-moving enemy, Bruneau lost twenty-eight more tanks and his division was virtually destroyed. 'It was sacrificed to stop a rout,' wrote an observer, 'sacrificed entirely in vain, for the rout goes on.'

Between Sedan and Namur, the 2nd Armoured Division never even went into action. Delayed by a fantastic muddle of orders and incompetent transport organisation, it was caught up in the general confusion as its units detrained at Hirson *en route* for the front. The 2nd was urgently needed for General Touchon's new army detachment, detailed to hold the German advance southwest of Sedan. Touchon's only other reliable formation was the still incomplete 14th Infantry Division. His others, all Ninth Army divisions, were so battered and depleted as to be useless. The non-arrival of the 2nd Armoured was thus a bitter blow for Touchon. After his line had been breached and one division almost annihilated in a four-hour battle, at 6pm Tassigny decided there was only one thing to do, withdraw south to the Aisne, between Attigny and Neufchâtel-sur-Aisne.

Thus, in this moment of emergency on the 15th May, France's armoured force had failed signally to arrest the Panzer onrush. Two-thirds of it (the 2nd and 3rd Divisions) were not even committed to battle. The whole handling of the French armour – indeed the notion of its role in battle –

was a grave indictment of French military thinking. The results of two decades of misconception were now in evidence. But even so, there was a slender chance that French armour might redeem itself. Command of a newly-projected 4th Armoured Division had just been given to a forward-looking professional soldier, who had long vainly advocated the formation of a French highly mobile armoured force, an offensive arm on the lines of the German Panzers: 50-year-old Colonel Charles de Gaulle.

That day de Gaulle, commander of the Fifth Army tanks in Alsace, was called to GHQ, Northeast, to receive instructions. Greeting him at Les Bondons, General George wryly reminded him: 'For you who have so long held the ideas which the enemy is putting into practice, here is the chance to act.' At Les Bondons de Gaulle detected an ominous atmosphere of strain. George seemed 'visibly overwhelmed', and though the staff was striving manfully to cope with the mounting burden of work, 'one could feel that hope was departing'.

Likewise at GHQ, Montry, there was gloom and pessimism. Officers had been tensely awaiting the outcome of the armoured divisions' intervention. The realisation that they had been ineffective brought deep disappointment. 'Nothing covers Paris any more,' recorded Captain Beaufre. ' . . . The battle appears irretrievably lost.' The grim mood had even permeated Supreme Headquarters, Vincennes, from which all pretence of confidence had now departed. There was 'a deathlike feeling' about the day, according to the officer Colonel Minart. The whole staff was on edge and anxious. In Gamelin, whose manner was as calm as ever, Minart claimed to detect a 'hidden and growing fear'.

Gamelin had much to worry him, not least an alarming report on the state of the Ninth Army from one of his personal staff, Colonel Guillaut. Guillaut had found the Ninth's position 'truly critical'. Corap's staff had lost touch with the divisions, and everywhere on the roads were troops fleeing at the sight of German motorcyclists or a few tanks. Gamelin was so dismayed that he decided to post Corap to the officers' reserve instead of giving him command of the Seventh Army. Guillaut's one encouraging sidelight was of the arrival of General Giraud to replace Corap. Giraud was a robust forceful commander who could inspire officers and men, and his presence had immediately raised the staff's drooping morale.

Unease about the battle situation was now spreading to various quarters in Paris. Press correspondents particularly, deprived of hard news, were worried about the true position on the Meuse front. That evening in the Press room at the War Ministry they learned something of the facts from the Ministry's official spokesman, Colonel Thomas. The Meuse, Colonel Thomas announced to a crowded gathering, had been crossed at Sedan. 'The situation is serious,' he added, 'but it is neither critical nor desperate.' But if not desperate, affairs were certainly critical. They seemed so to Paul Reynaud who, in his office at the Quai d'Orsay, now gave vent to his acute concern at Gamelin's leadership. Learning of the collapse of the Meuse armies he was flabbergasted to hear from Daladier that Gamelin had no countermeasures to propose. 'Ah! If only Pétain were here,' he exclaimed (thinking of France's great soldier-hero, who was then in Madrid as French Ambassador to Spain) 'he would be able to influence Gamelin.'

Reynaud and his colleague were becoming increasingly fearful about the fate of Paris. The capital seemed to them the obvious objective for the German armoured columns now racing unresisted into Northern France. At that moment Reinhardt's and Guderian's leading Panzers were hardly more than 120 miles away. Inadequately briefed by Supreme

Headquarters, Vincennes (a standing grievance of Reynaud's), the Premier's fears were intensified by a 'telephoned SOS' from Daladier, so much so that at 7pm he launched a dramatic appeal, the third in twenty-four hours, to Winston Churchill in London: 'We lost the battle last night. The road to Paris is open. Send us all aircraft and troops you can.'

That night, as Parisians peaceably dined and slept, blissfully unaware of the danger threatening them, the French leaders expected the imminent fall of Paris. The telephone lines between the capital and Vincennes buzzed with tense messages. At 8.30 Gamelin called Daladier at the War Office to announce the reported passage of German tanks between Rethel and Laon. Daladier was incredulous. It was impossible, he declared. Then

Above: The ordeal of the refugees. *Below:* Daily the news gets worse

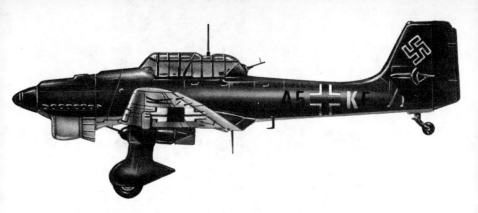

The Junkers Ju 87
Specification for the Ju 87B-2: *Engine:* Junkers Jumo 211, developing
1,200 horse power for take off. *Armament:* either one 1,100 pound bomb or
one 550 and four 110 pound bombs; three 7.9mm machine guns.
Maximum speed: 238 mph at 13,400 feet. *Ceiling:* 26,200 feet.
Range: 370 miles with a 1,100 pounds bomb. *Weights:* empty, 5,980 pounds;
loaded, 9,560 pounds. *Span:* 45 feet 3½ inches. *Length:* 36 feet 5 inches

The Somua S-35 tank
With the Char-B, the Somua S-35 equipped the more modern elements of the
French armoured forces, and was fast for its size. Specification: *Weight:* 20 tons.
Armament: one 47mm gun and one 7.5mm machine gun. *Crew:* 3 men.
Maximum speed: 25 mph. *Armour:* 55mm maximum. *Engine:* 190 hp.
Length: 17 feet 4¾ inches. *Width:* 6 feet 11½ inches

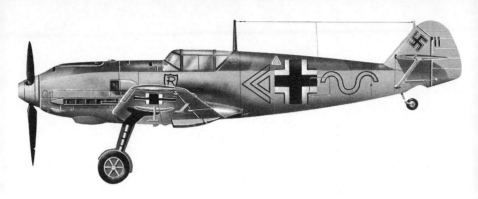

Me-109E-3
Engine: Daimler-Benz 601A, 1,100 hp. *Armament:* 2 x 7.9mm machine guns and 3 x 20mm cannon. *Speed:* 354 mph at 12,300 ft. *Ceiling:* 37,500 ft. *Range:* 412 miles. *Weights:* 4,421 lbs empty and 5,523 lbs loaded. *Span:* 32 ft 4½ ins. *Length:* 28 ft 3 ins

The Char-B tank
The Char-B, the best tank in service with the French armoured forces at the time of the German invasion, had armour twice as thick as that on German tanks, as did the Somua, and carried a heavy armament, but was hampered in action by having only a one-man turret. Specification: *Weight:* 32 tons. *Armament:* one 75mm gun, one 47mm gun and two 7.5mm machine guns. *Crew:* 4 men. *Maximum speed:* 17½ mph. *Armour:* 60mm maximum. *Engine:* 300 hp. *Length:* 21 feet 4¾ inches. *Width:* 8 feet 2½ inches

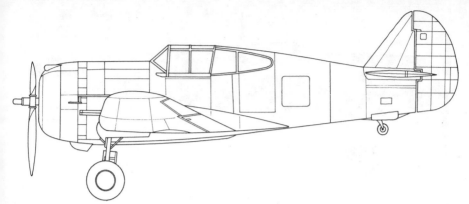

The Curtiss Hawk 75A was one of the best fighters flown by the French in 1940, but was underarmoured and underarmed by contemporary German and British standards, and consequently suffered heavy losses. *Engine:* Pratt & Whitney R-1830, 1,050hp at 10,000 feet. *Armament:* one .5-inch and one .3-inch machine gun. *Maximum speed:* 313mph at 10,000 feet. *Rate of climb:* 4.8 minutes to 15,000 feet. *Ceiling:* 33,000 feet. *Range:* 825 miles. *Weights empty/loaded:* 4,567/5,470 lbs. *Span:* 37 feet 4 inches. *Length:* 28 feet 6 inches

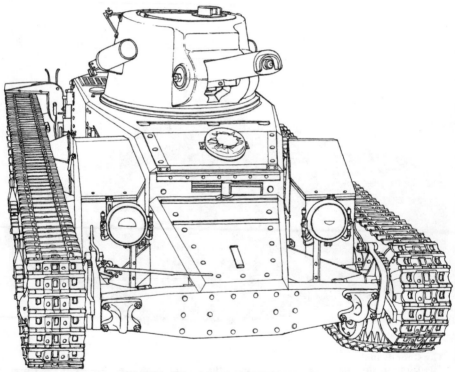

The British Infantry Tank Mark 1 was, like the French Char B, hampered in action by its one-man turret. Although its firepower was light, the armour was able to prevent the penetration of any shell a German tank could use. *Weight:* 11 tons. *Crew:* 2. *Armament:* one .5 or .303-inch machine gun. *Armour:* $2\frac{1}{2}$ inches maximum, .36 inches minimum. *Maximum speed:* 8mph (road). *Engine:* Ford V-8, 70bhp. *Length:* 16 feet $3\frac{1}{4}$ inches. *Width:* 7 feet 8 inches. *Height:* 6 feet 7 inches

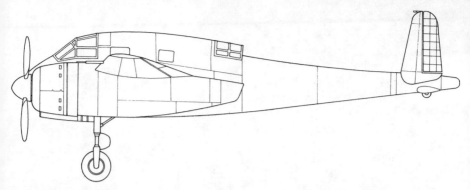

The Breguet 691 was one of the best of the French light attack bombers available at the time of the German invasion but like other good French aircraft, it was not available in sufficient numbers. *Engine:* Hispano-Suiza 14AB radials, 725hp at 10,660 feet. *Armament:* one 20mm cannon and four 7.5mm machine guns plus eight 110-lb bombs. *Maximum speed:* 298mph at 13,120 feet. *Rate of climb:* 7 minutes to 13,120 feet. *Range:* 840 miles. *Weights empty/loaded:* 6,834/11,023 lbs. *Span:* 50 feet 5 inches. *Length:* 31 feet 8¾ inches

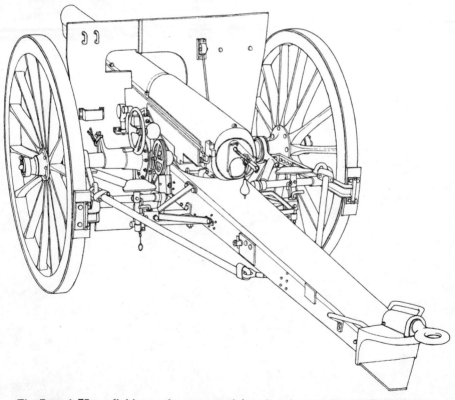

The French 75mm field gun, the same model as that they used in the First World War, was not adequate to halt the onrush of the German tank divisions in the Second World War. Its range was over 12,000 yards and its rate of fire about fifteen rounds a minute

The advancing Germans find no opposition

he pressed Gamelin to attack at once. 'Attack? What with?' replied Gamelin. I've no more reserves . . . Between Laon and Paris I've not got a single body of troops.' At this, Daladier (as recorded by William C Bullitt, the US Ambassador to France, who just then was visiting Daladier) seemed to shrink visibly. 'So, it means the destruction of the French Army,' he asked finally. 'Yes, it's the destruction of the French Army,' replied Gamelin.

So alarmed was Supreme Headquarters about the fate of Paris that during the night a Vincennes staff officer telephoned the Paris Police Prefect, Roger Langeron, to ask how many *gardes mobiles* and trucks he had available. The road to Paris was open, said the officer and must be barred at all costs. Langeron replied that most of the *gardes mobiles* were mobilized, but those he had were at the army's disposal.

At 2.30am Paul Baudouin, the War Cabinet Secretary, was roused by a telephone call announcing that German armoured forces were near Laon 'and Paris might well fall during the course of the day'. Baudouin was told to dress, pack and await instructions. Meanwhile, in the office of the Minister of the Interior, an emergency conference was being held, attended by Reynaud, Daladier, the Paris Military Governor, General Gamelin, Langeron, and others. At this, as Reynaud later told Baudouin (with dubious accuracy), 'Daladier was broken down, and General Hering, in a state of collapse, had advised the Government to leave Paris without delay.' Gamelin, moreover, had disclaimed all responsibility for Paris beyond the coming evening, Thursday 16th May.

On that fateful 15th May, the day of the German armoured breakout from the Meuse, French leadership, both civil and military, had showed signs of disarray that boded ill for the coming weeks of intensifying crisis.

The end of their troubles

Weygand replaces Gamelin

In view of the situation on the Meuse front, it was now plain that Plan D was a dead letter. The only hope for the Allied armies in central Belgium, if they were to avoid being trapped and surrounded, was to withdraw immediately. But even now the High Command's reaction was dangerously slow: it was not until the 16th that the general retirement order was issued, to take effect on the night of the 16th-17th. Meanwhile, early on the 16th, Gamelin was showing his concern for the armoured threat to Paris by issuing to his commanders an order to 'form kernels of resistance' against the advancing Panzers. And to protect Paris itself he was recalling forty squads of *gardes mobiles* from the army and arranging for troop reinforcements.

Among the Government, likewise, alarm still ran high as stories of a German armoured thrust towards Paris persisted. Reynaud now faced the problem of whether or not to order the evacuation of the Government and ministries. At a noon meeting in his office it was agreed to defer a final decision. At the same time, as an index of the prevailing mood, a wholesale burning of official documents was taking place in the courtyard of the Foreign Ministry on the Quai d'Orsay, allegedly on the orders of the Secretary-General of the Ministry. From every window the files and archives showered down, jettisoned by sailors from the Ministry of Marine. Flustered clerks fed them onto the pyre. The bonfire continued all day, shooting its charred fragments over astonished passers-by.

According to a French Senator, then in Paris, this was the day that the capital suddenly took on a war-like aspect. Within almost a single hour that morning, buses and taxis vanished from the streets, commandeered to transport troops and refugees. Private car traffic increased as people began to leave Paris. At last Parisians, too long misled, were beginning to grasp the truth about the military position. 'There is panic in the air,' commented a British journalist. In the Palais-Bourbon, the Chamber of Deputies (equivalent to the British House of Commons) buzzed with alarmist rumours about the advancing Germans, panicking French divisions, and the Government's plans

Marshal Pétain, who was to succeed Reynaud as French premier

for immediate evacuation. Amid this hysteria Reynaud arrived to address the House at 3.30pm. Declaring categorically that the Government would stay in Paris, he added significantly: '... perhaps we shall have to change methods and men.'

Away in the rear of the Meuse front, the great rout was continuing. Masses of disordered troops were converging on Compiègne, eighty miles behind the river. Before noon some 20,000 Ninth Army men had reached there and the figure was still growing. And eastward of the Ninth Army, the Second Army was likewise straggling back in confusion. That morning at Dizy-le-Gros, fifteen miles north of Neufchâtel -sur-Aisne, a tank unit moving north came upon a ragged column of Huntziger's men, 'hopeless, gaunt, dazed with fatigue', limping away from the front, led by a distracted officer who inveighed against the overwhelming enemy air power. In places the exodus was even nearing Paris, whose outskirts were suddenly full of men who had lost their units and officers. And along with them trekked the huge procession of refugees from the Pas-de-Calais, Nord and Ardennes departments, effectively blocking the northbound military traffic.

For the first time, in this day, the 16th, the French communiqué spoke of a 'war of movement'. And indeed almost the whole front, from central Belgium to the reaches of the Aisne, was now shifting back in varying stages of order and disorder. In some areas a front hardly existed at all, notably in what was still nominally the Ninth Army zone. From Philippeville southward, with most contact and communication severed, isolated commanders were striving desperately to assemble odd groups of men on emergency defence lines inside France. Not even the energetic Giraud, the Ninth's new commander, could save this ill-starred army. In their retreat some units had more than their share of misfortune – like the exhausted survivors of the 22nd Division who took over the defences at Anor and Saint-Michel only to find the blockhouses unequipped and without doors, their automatic weapons unusable and apparently sabotaged.

As the left-flank formations of the Second Army evaporated along with the right-flank formations of the Ninth, and General Touchon's force found itself outflanked or wrongly placed to be effective, the huge gap created by Reinhardt's and Guderian's Panzers was left almost devoid of French troops. And by that evening Reinhardt's leading tanks had rolled through Vervins and Guise to reach the Oise. But, on paper, still in a position to oppose Guderian's tanks was the French 2nd Armoured Division, uncommitted on the previous day. The 2nd, however, was again to be frustrated: after an inexplicable cancellation of its subsequent order to counterattack at Montcornet, it was allotted the purely defensive role of holding the crossings of the Oise and the Sambre canal. And now, to confront Guderian's tanks advancing between Guise and La Fère, all that could be marshalled at once were some fifty tanks.

The only French tank commander with offensive ideas that day seemed to be de Gaulle, entrusted with the formation of the new 4th Armoured Division and promoted to General. De Gaulle spent the day reconnoitring near the Sissonne canal. He noted that the German forces debouching from the Ardennes were moving, not southwards, but westwards towards Saint-Quentin. Watching the enemy's unhindered progress, de Gaulle made a solemn resolve: 'I will fight . . . until the enemy is defeated and the national stain washed clean.'

In London, as the Meuse disaster had developed, there had been little clear knowledge as to what was really happening. In view of Reynaud's three appeals for fighter aid and more than one request from Gamelin, the position seemed grave, but exactly how grave the British War Cabinet could not be certain. To Winston Churchill, therefore, this seemed the time to go and find out: and on the afternoon of the 16th he flew to Paris with the Vice-Chief of the Imperial General Staff, General Sir John Dill, and the Assistant Secretary to the War Cabinet, General Ismay, for the first of the crucial Anglo-French conferences that were to mark the coming weeks.

The meeting took place in Reynaud's office at the Quai d'Orsay. Other senior officers had joined Churchill, and the French party comprised Reynaud, Daladier, Gamelin, and others. If Churchill was unaware of the real situation before, he was now left in no doubt of it. Standing before a large map, Gamelin presented the full gloomy picture of the German breakthrough. Churchill then asked 'Where is the strategic reserve?', to be greeted with Gamelin's bleak answer 'There is none.' 'I was dumbfounded,' recorded Churchill.

Characteristically he did all he could to bolster the Frenchmen's fighting spirit, pressing for a counterstroke against the German salient. But, shrugging hopelessly, Gamelin pleaded inferiority of numbers, equipment and method. He then stressed the urgent need for British air support,

to which Churchill replied that Britain was fully stretched for home defence. Returning to the British Embassy, he nevertheless cabled the War Cabinet asking authorisation for the transfer to France of six more fighter squadrons. At 11.30pm the reply arrived: the Cabinet agreed. Churchill drove forthwith to Reynaud's private flat in the Place du Palais Bourbon to inform the French Premier. Reynaud, roused from bed, shook his hand in silent thanks.

But at Supreme Headquarters, according to the staff officer Colonel Minart, an almost panic mood now prevailed. Files were being packed, maps removed, and officers hurriedly preparing for departure. Gamelin's Chief of Staff had even had a 75mm gun installed at the north entrance to the fort. And Gamelin himself, noted Minart, appeared worried. 'No one dares to approach him,' wrote the Colonel. 'It is indeed a lost battle.'

Nevertheless, next day (the 17th) Gamelin was at least relieved of one anxiety. As the Panzer columns continued their advance, it was clear that they were moving away from Paris. For the moment the capital was reprieved. But Gamelin could be under no illusion about the magnitude of the German threat as the enemy armour pressed on into the heart of northern France. In the south the 1st Panzers of Guderian's XIX Armoured Corps, flanked as before by the 2nd and 10th, were nearing the Oise in two groups. In the centre the 6th and 8th Armoured Divisions of Reinhardt's XLI Corps were advancing on the Oise via Rumigny and Vervins. Behind these two corps followed the three divisions of the 14th Motorized Corps. In the north were General Hoth's 5th and 7th Armoured Divisions, entrusted with the vital role of outflanking the Allied armies in Belgium by reaching the line Maubeuge-Cambrai-Arras. These would be reinforced next day by the 3rd and 4th Armoured Divisions of the XVI Armoured Corps, transferred from

General von Bock's Army Group B. Within twenty-four hours nine German Panzer divisions would be driving through the great hiatus left open by France's shattered Ninth and Second Armies.

On this eighth day of the great battle there were ominous signs that the whole Allied strategy was beginning to founder. Hustled by Reichenau's forces, the BEF and French First Army were making their fighting retreat to the river Escaut (Scheldt). The roads of Belgium and northern France were congested by hordes of refugees. And the High Command now realised that south of the French frontier the German armoured advance was directed to Amiens and probably the Channel. As Georges now sought to throw a screen of divisions along the Somme and the Aisne, Gamelin was envisaging a counterattack to enable the Somme forces to join up with those in the north while time still remained. For this purpose he was forming a new Seventh Army, to be led by General Frère, a corps commander in the Fifth Army.

To match the gravity of the situation, on that day Gamelin issued a stark Order: 'The fate of the country, that of our allies, and the destinies of the world hang upon the battle now in progress . . . Conquer or die. We must conquer.' But now Gamelin's own days as Supreme Commander were numbered. Reynaud, who had never believed in his Dyle Plan or trusted his military leadership, had decided to replace him with the 73-year-old General Maxime Weygand. Recalled from retirement at the war's start after serving earlier as French C-in-C, Weygand was currently C-in-C in the Near East. Though he had never held a field command, being essentially a staff officer, Reynaud admired him greatly for his fighting spirit and his connection in the First World War with the great Marshal Foch. He now believed that Weygand, if anyone, could save the situation. So that

morning he telegraphed Weygand at Beirut urgently requesting his return to France.

As yet Gamelin was unaware of Reynaud's move. There was indeed irony in the fact that, under the shadow of dismissal himself, he was remarking on General Georges' growing inability to handle affairs at GHQ Northeast. Visiting Georges on the 18th, he noted the chaotic state of the Les Bondons offices (so different from the cloister-like calm of Vincennes) and Georges' harassing working conditions. He spoke of this to Doumenc, who told him that he (Gamelin) would have to assume control of affairs himself. 'Just warn me of the right moment,' Gamelin replied.

Meanwhile Reynaud was taking another step to strengthen France's war-effort. On the 15th he had asked that revered national figure, Marshal Pétain, to return to France from Madrid to join his Government as Minister of State and Vice-President of the Council. Pétain had agreed, arriving in Paris early on the 18th. Reynaud hastened to induct the 84-year-old Marshal into the military situation. That afternoon he escorted him to both Georges' and Gamelin's headquarters for top-level briefing. As Pétain left Gamelin he gave him an affectionate hand. 'I pity you with all my heart,' he said.

Gamelin's final act of command was to take place next day, the 19th. At 5am that morning Doumenc telephoned him at Vincennes. 'I have the clear impression that the moment has come for you to intervene,' he said. Three hours later Colonel Minart, acting as Gamelin's liaison officer, arrived at Georges' command post. Doumenc told him tersely: 'General Gamelin must take over command.' Gamelin's own car then arrived and, short and stocky, he strode into the house to meet Georges, who looked tired and depressed. After a brief talk Gamelin told him that, as Supreme Commander, he thought it necessary to draw up the general strategic plan

Above: A British anti-tank barrier. *Below:* The prisoners stream back
Right: Confrontation of enemies

that was now indicated, and was shown by Georges to a first-floor room. There he carefully wrote out his 'Personal and Secret Instruction No 12'.

This five-paragraph Instruction, diffidently beginning 'Without wishing to intervene in the conduct of the battle in progress', specified, in brief, an Allied assault across the German Panzer corridor so as to pinch off the leading enemy armoured forces and free 1st Army Group from encirclement. It ended: 'Everything is a matter of hours.' Gamelin signed the order at 9.45am and then, in the downstairs salon, read it to Georges, General Vuillemin, C-in-C, French Air Force, and other officers. Both signified their approval. Gamelin told them that if the plan failed, he thought it would be hard to defend metropolitan France. Soon after, he received a message that Weygand was due to arrive in Paris that morning. This was his first intimation of his own replacement.

General Weygand landed at Etampes airfield, thirty-five miles southwest of Paris, soon after mid-day – somewhat inauspiciously, for as his plane touched down it pancaked across the airfield. The general climbed out unhurt and drove to Paris. At the War Ministry, alert and spruce in his impeccable uniform, he saw Reynaud, who offered him the Supreme Command. Before accepting, Weygand asked to visit Gamelin's and Georges' command posts. Meeting Gamelin in his underground Vincennes office, he was struck by his air of strain. Gamelin explained to him his Instruction of that morning, with which Weygand was 'entirely in agreement'. At Les Bondons, Weygand was even more shocked by Georges' changed appearance and the despondency of the staff. By the time he returned to Paris he had determined to accept the proffered appointment.

Reynaud, who had been joined at the War Ministry by Marshal Pétain, was delighted to learn of Weygand's

decision. In accepting the appointment, Weygand was in fact being given greater powers than Gamelin had possessed, for he was now nominated Chief of Staff of National Defence, C-in-C of all theatres of operations. Asked by Paul Baudouin, as he left the room, of his first impression of events, Weygand replied: 'Bad. The position is grave, but one must not despair.'

In his office at Vincennes, General Maurice Gamelin now awaited only the formal notification of his replacement. This academic, philosophically-minded general had staked his reputation on a strategy that had failed. Furthermore, the unwieldy and ambiguous structure of the High Command – as fashioned by Gamelin himself – had aggravated that failure, by leaving the C-in-C Northeast less closely supported by the Supreme Commander in times of emergency than was needful, though Gamelin was always to maintain that he had interpreted the role of Supreme Commander correctly. But now he passed his last hours at Vincennes against a background of something like panic. Colonel Minart, returning from a depressing day at Doumenc's and Georges' headquarters, in which he had gathered that Gamelin's Instruction was already dead, found the command post apparently in the throes of removal. He tried vainly to persuade Gamelin to appoint Huntziger in Georges' place. As the general raised his hands in a helpless gesture Minart felt that he was speaking to a defeated man.

That night Gamelin received official word of his fate. 'I wish General Weygand greater success than I've had,' he remarked drily to his aides. By ten next morning, with little fuss or notice, he had left Vincennes for his modest Paris apartment after just eleven days of supreme command in the Western offensive.

To the German infantryman marching in the sunshine it all seemed so easy

Counterstroke
abandoned

Gamelin's successor, General Weygand, was incisive, brisk and markedly energetic for his seventy-three years. On the jaded officers of GHQ, Montry, where he held his first conference on the afternoon of the 20th, this trim-figured soldier made a welcome impression, promising a firmer, tighter control of affairs. One of his first acts was to establish closer contact with General Georges, who, as he thought, had been inadequately supported by Gamelin. His immediate plan, based on Gamelin's Instruction No 12, was to unite the southern and northern forces and seal off the enemy Panzer spearheads by means of concerted attacks in the Arras-Amiens area. On the 20th he ordered 1st Army Group to strike southwards and fight 'like dogs'. But events were already outpacing him, for that day Guderian's westward-racing tanks took Amiens and reached Abbeville at the mouth of the Somme.

Now, with the Germans at the Channel and the million-strong Allied forces in the north cut off from the French armies in the south, began the second phase of the campaign – the battle of Flanders and Picardy. For General Weygand, fatally handicapped by being called in too late, it could promise little but frustration and virtually certain defeat. He learned for himself the predicament of the northern armies when he visited Ypres on the 21st to confer with the Allied commanders. It was here arranged for the carrying-out of his counterattack plan and an Allied withdrawal westwards if this should fail. The meeting was followed by tragedy, in the death of General Billotte as a result of a traffic accident. Returning in the dark to his Béthune headquarters, along crowded roads, he was fatally injured. He was replaced as 1st Army Group commander by General Blanchard of the French First Army.

Blanchard now took on a dauntingly heavy task. He was assuming command of a force that was rapidly losing cohesion in its enforced retreat westwards. For some days Billotte, overwhelmed by events, had ceased to exercise effective control on the group. Lord Gort, commanding the BEF, was so perturbed at the lack of communication from Army Group HQ that he was contemplating having to take his own decisions – even as to withdrawing his nine divisions to the coast. On the 19th he had so informed the War Cabinet in London. The Cabinet disliked the idea, favouring instead a southward push by the BEF to the Somme. General Ironside, CIGS, was forthwith sent to Belgium to appraise Gort. Gort, however, opposed the southward move as being impracticable, and Ironside, who agreed with him, reported thus to the British Cabinet late on the 21st. A major dilemma now faced the Cabinet: should the BEF, alone or with its allies, drive south for the Somme, or should it attempt the grave alternative – retirement to the coast and eventual evacuation?

To resolve this issue, on 22nd May Churchill made his second visit to France. With colleagues he met Reynaud and Weygand at Vincennes. The British Premier, welcoming Weygand's aggressive attitude, was glad to find that the general's ideas for a southward thrust coincided with his own. He straightway drafted a résumé of the meeting's decisions, which stated, *inter alia:* 'The British Army and the French First Army should attack southwest towards Bapaume and Cambrai at the earliest moment . . . The new French Army Group which is advancing upon Amiens and forming a line along the Somme should strike northwards and join hands with the British divisions who are attacking in the direction of Bapaume.'

If the Weygand plan seemed theoretically practicable, it was ignoring one important factor: the ability of the troops to carry it out. 'But men are made of flesh and blood,' remarked Captain Beaufre, of these sore-tried northern troops. For over ten days the Franco-British armies had been almost continuously on the move. They had hardly reached their positions when they were forced to retreat. Pressed by the enemy, hampered by hordes of refugees, they were now menaced from the rear by the tank columns driving up the Channel coast. The plan presented a further drawback: by specifying that 'the Belgian Army should withdraw to the line of the Yser' (Belgium's most westerly river line) it not only demanded the impossible of the Belgians by requiring them to abandon all their material and supplies, based to the east of the Yser, but it asked them to sever connection with the BEF, on their right flank. If this happened, the Germans would, as King Leopold, the Belgian Army's C-in-C, was forcibly and repeatedly to point out, drive a wedge between the Belgians and British, with disastrous results. It had also to be remembered that the Belgian Army was purely a national defence force, not equipped to fight outside Belgian territory.

In fact, at this vital juncture, as Blanchard replaced the late General Billotte at 1st Army Group, no coordinated counterblow from the north was made. Blanchard, a military theoretician rather than a fighting general, was, like Weygand, inheriting a hopeless situation. The most dynamic commander would have found it impossible to marshal his forces for the southward thrust. On the 21st a limited and only briefly successful Anglo-French attack was made at Arras. On the 24th Gort and Blanchard arranged to launch a concerted assault two days later, though this never materialised owing to the increasingly fluid state of the Anglo-Belgian front.

But besides the harassed Blanchard's own difficulties of command control and liaison, there were exterior factors jeopardising 1st Army Group's survival as the German ring tightened

German dispatch riders at the Aisne

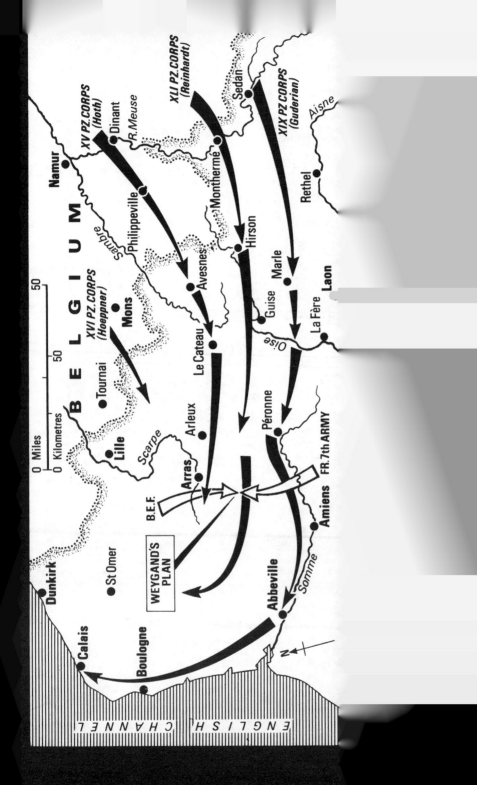

round it: the top-level misconception of the situation, and attempts at remote control, the indecision, the mutual misunderstanding and poor communication, all bedevilled by the conflicting national interests that now began to emerge.

From the BEF's viewpoint, if 1st Army Group's junction with the southern armies proved impossible, the only hope for the British was to disengage and evacuate by sea. Churchill was thinking thus when, on the afternoon of the 23rd, he asked Reynaud whether, in the circumstances, the BEF should not retreat towards the coast. Weygand was satisfied, and nothing need be changed, replied Reynaud. But despite this assurance, the British War Cabinet, following the receipt of a discouraging signal from Gort, was worried by the apparent lack of Allied co-ordination. Churchill cabled his misgivings to Reynaud. This incensed Weygand, who now seemingly suspected the BEF of preparing to abandon his plan.

But Weygand himself now appeared to be doubting the plan's efficacy, for on the 24th he told Reynaud and Pétain that he had had to modify it (bringing the north-south junction farther east) because the British had withdrawn from Arras unnecessarily and were making for the Channel ports. He later clinched the matter with a note to Reynaud: ' . . . I have directed the Commander of Number One Army Group, if he considers the manoeuvre previously ordered can no longer be carried out, to form a bridgehead as extensive as possible in front of the three northern ports (Dunkirk, Gravelines and Ostend).' Within four days of its inauguration the Weygand Plan was dead.

That day for the first time Weygand had let fall the dread word 'capitulation'. When reporting to Reynaud and Pétain he had said that unless the junction were achieved quickly, it would be hard to avoid the capitulation of the northern armies, running short, as they were, of food and ammunition. Regarding the remaining French forces (the southern armies) which would be in position along the Somme, the Ailette canal and the Aisne, these too would find it difficult to resist a German assault if the northern armies were defeated. Nevertheless, he told Paul Baudouin at Supreme Headquarters that evening, when French resistance on the Somme and Aisne had been broken, 'what is left of the French Army should continue to fight where it stands until it is annihilated.'

While Weygand reflected thus gloomily, Hitler was having very different thoughts. Contemplating with high satisfaction the perfect execution of his plans up to this time, he now, on the 24th, issued from Führer Headquarters his plain and unambiguous order for total victory – Directive No 13, in which he declared the next German aim to be the annihilation of the Allied forces surrounded in Flanders. 'The Army will then,' he added, 'prepare to destroy in the shortest possible time the remaining enemy forces in France.'

The inability of the French 1st Army (now commanded by General Prioux in place of Blanchard) to stage any kind of offensive was confirmed on the 25th, when a staff officer from 1st Army Group, Major Fauvelle, reported to a meeting of the War Cabinet, held at noon in Reynaud's War Ministry office. Fauvelle, badly demoralized, described how the troops were 'stupefied' by bombing, were without bread and were gravely short of heavy guns and ammunition. The British, he said, were preparing to evacuate and the Belgians had little fighting capacity left. Early surrender was unavoidable, he declared. Impressed by this chilling testimony, Weygand ordered Fauvelle to return immediately to Blanchard, with the message that it was for Blanchard to decide whether to try the southward breakthrough or retire to the Channel ports.

That evening, at the Elysée Palace,

France's War Committee (comprising the nation's political and service leaders) met for two hours to discuss the crisis. The tone was one of un-alloyed gloom. Weygand presented a bleak picture of future military prospects, holding out little hope that, after the surrender of the northern armies, the Somme-Aisne line could be successfully defended. Reynaud spoke of saving the army's hour by 'a fight to the death'. From President Lebrun came an ominous reference to the possibility of a peace offer from Germany, though he admitted that France had undertaken not to sign a separate peace. Reynaud pointed out that in the event of such an offer Britain would have to be consulted. The aged Marshal Pétain then intervened to air a long-standing grudge about unequal Franco-British sacrifice. More constructively, Rey-naud promised to visit London next day to consult the British War Cabinet. The most significant thing about this meeting was that it revealed the first signs of the rift that was forming between the 'fight-on-at-all-costs' and 'separate-peace-with-Germany' factions among France's leaders.

At this juncture Weygand was facing a double disappointment. Not only had his plan been frustrated by the failure of the northern armies to strike southwards: the southern forces were failing to launch their blow to the north. Ranged behind the river lines from the Channel to the Aisne were the bulk of three armies – the newly formed 3rd Army Group of General Besson, comprising (from west to east) General Robert Altmayer's Tenth Army Detachment, Frère's Seventh Army and Touchon's Sixth Army. The Weygand Plan had provided for the northward strike to be made by the Seventh Army, but as this had not materialized by the 25th, Weygand was regretfully writing it off, citing General Frère's 'increasing difficulties' in providing an attacking force and completing the defence of

the Lower Somme. By this failure a great opportunity may have been lost; for behind the leading Panzer groups and their accompanying motorized divisions, as they raced for the Channel coast, stretched a vacuum that would have been highly vulner-able to Allied attack until it could be filled by following infantry.

There was one exception to 3rd Army Group's inactivity. For three days, from the 26th, the newly formed 4th Armoured Division (part of Altmayer's Tenth Army Detachment) vigorously attacked the strong enemy bridgehead south of Abbeville. General de Gaulle's division now amounted to 140 fully operational tanks and six infantry battalions, supported by six artillery groups. In the first two assaults de Gaulle gained two of his three objectives, though with the loss of a third of his tanks. When battle was resumed on the 29th

the Germans had received reinforcements, as had de Gaulle himself. That evening his troops drove on to the foot of the formidable Mont Caubert, but without the air support de Gaulle had requested they failed to reach the summit. Next day the 4th was relieved by the BEF's 51st Scottish Division (General Fortune). The operation was successful in that the German bridgehead was greatly reduced and (according to de Gaulle) the enemy could no longer 'debouch from it in force'.

While abandoning the idea of a massive northward strike, Weygand was now concentrating increasingly on the battle which he knew would shortly be forced on Besson's 3rd Army Group – the crucial battle for France herself. This, he foresaw, would be launched as soon as the Germans had had time to regroup after completing the defeat of northern

The pitiful trek continues

armies. To nerve the troops on the Somme-Aisne river line for the coming struggle he issued, on the 26th May, a General Order which began: 'The battle on which depends the fate of the country will be fought without thought of retreat on the position we occupy at present. All commanders . . . must be animated by the fierce resolve to fight to the death where they stand.'

But along with its stirring exhortations the Order contained directions for a significantly novel tactic – as foreshadowed by Gamelin on the 16th when he spoke of 'kernels of resistance'. 'All behind the principal line (continued Weygand's Order), from the front to the greatest depth possible, must be organized in a chequerwork of centres of resistance . . . ' This instruction for defence in depth was, for the French, revolutionary: it signalled the departure from the classic principle of linear defence on which the French Army had long relied. How far it would be' possible to prepare for the new tactic and adhere to it in the heat and pressure of the forthcoming battle remained to be seen.

Meanwhile events on the northern front were going from bad to worse. The last concerted resistance of 1st Army Group was collapsing. Late on the 24th the Belgian IV Corps, positioned on the Lys, was pushed back on a twelve-mile front between Courtrai and Menin. Lord Gort, on the Belgians' right, thus found himself in a dangerous situation, with his forces theatened with separation from them at Menin, the Anglo-Belgian junction point. Moreover, he foresaw

The Germans across the Aisne

the Belgians being forced to retire not west but north, so increasing the gap that would be opened between the two armies. By now (the 25th) all thought of any southward attack had been finally forsaken, and that evening Gort became so alarmed at the widening gap between himself and the Belgians that he resolved to withdraw to cover Ypres.

The Belgians were now facing imminent disaster. When Blanchard, anxiously intent on plugging the breach around Courtrai, visited Belgian GHQ at Bruges on the 26th to stiffen their faltering opposition, King Leopold declared that he had used all his reserves and his troops were unable to launch a further attack. He appealed instead for a Franco-British counterthrust in the threatened sector – a plea endorsed by the Belgian Chief of Staff, General Michiels, who sent Gort an urgent

call for immediate support. Linked with this SOS was an ominous warning from the Belgian High Command to General Weygand 'that the situation of the Belgian Army is grave. The High Command intends to continue the struggle to the extremity of its resources . . . The limits of Belgian resistance have very nearly been reached.' In the face of the Belgian plight, that evening Blanchard had to tell King Leopold that the BEF would be unable to attack at Courtrai and would be abandoning its line (on the Belgian right) for a more westerly position covering Ypres and Lille.

On the BEF's right, the French First Army was likewise raggedly retreating. Typical of its hard-pressed formations was the 2nd North African Division, which on the 26th was just north of Douai. The 2nd North African was withdrawing at the rate of some twenty miles a night. In violent

actions on the Dyle and elsewhere it had suffered heavy losses, with its regiment, originally 3,000 strong, reduced to some 1,300 men. Next day, under continuous attack, the division fought its way back across the Lys. The men's spirit remained high. The commander of an armoured unit told a fellow-officer: 'At two to one we should have had the Boche as easy as winking. But four to one, what can you do?'

On the 26th May Weygand made one final attempt to control events in the north. In answer to a request from Blanchard for an 'authorized co-ordinator' to overcome command difficulties, he sent General Doumenc's deputy, General Koeltz, to Blanchard as his personal agent. In particular, Koeltz was to arrange for the largest practicable bridgehead in the Dunkirk area. At a meeting next day at the small hilltop town of Cassel, twenty miles south of Dunkirk, attended by Koeltz, Blanchard, Admiral Abrial (in charge at Dunkirk), two French and two British generals, it was agreed that, as Dunkirk was of doubtful use on account of bombing, the occupation of Gravelines should be reinforced and Calais occupied if possible. But such was the speed of the German advance that this latter decision was already outdated, for Calais had fallen the day before.

For the rest, Weygand was now confined to issuing fighting appeals to his isolated northern commanders. From Vincennes he radioed Gort on the 25th: 'The British Army should participate vigorously in the necessary general counterattacks. The situation demands hard hitting.' He likewise sent a strongly worded message to King Leopold. But he continued, it seemed, to be less than appreciative of the immense difficulties with which these commanders were contending. Two days later, at Reynaud's mid-day conference, he told the Premier: 'Not only do the English not attack, but they retreat, and the Belgians are giving way.'

British
evacuation
and Belgian
surrender

The Belgians were indeed giving way, and now they were not long to remain in the battle. At 4am on the 28th May, after eighteen days' determined and increasingly desperate resistance, the Belgian Army laid down its arms. Retreating continuously in conformity with Allied orders and with most of its country over-run and war material abandoned, it had no choice but to surrender. Its fate had been sealed more than ten days earlier by the French collapse on the Meuse which had signalled the eclipse of 1st Army Group. Like Lord Gort, King Leopold, as Belgian C-in-C, had frequently found himself hampered by bad communications, lack of adequate directives and High Command indecision. Militarily the Belgian Army's capitulation made little difference to the overall Allied situation, and its inevitability had been clear for some days. Nevertheless, despite the stubborn fight put up by the Belgians and the numerous warnings issued by King Leopold, the King was to be violently and unfairly condemned for the surrender – particularly by his French allies.

When General Weygand, in conference with Generals Georges, Doumenc and Besson at Vincennes, received a signal from GHQ Northeast on the 27th May that King Leopold was inquiring surrender conditions of the Germans and was proposing a cease-fire beginning at midnight, 'the news,' he wrote later, 'came like a thunderclap.' In a reply to GHQ Northeast he called the King's move an 'act of desertion'. Within an hour he was at Reynaud's office where, at a tense meeting attended by the Premier, Pétain, senior Belgian Ministers (now in Paris) and later British representatives, Reynaud bitterly attacked Leopold for his abandonment of the Allies, failure to warn them of his action, and consequent risking of the whole Allied position. The immediate Franco-British reaction to the surrender approach was made clear by the statement issued at the meeting's close: 'The French and British Governments agree to instruct their Commanders-in-Chief to defend the honour of their flags by dissociating themselves entirely from the Belgian armistice.'

At 8am next morning Frenchmen were shocked and dismayed to hear their Premier, making a national radio broadcast, announce the capitulation in these terms: 'I have to announce a grave event to the French people. This took place during the night. France can no longer count on the assistance of the Belgian Army . . . It is this Belgian Army which has suddenly surrendered unconditionally at the height of battle at the orders of its King, without warning its French and British comrades . . . Now, in the full course of battle, without any warning to General Blanchard, without, indeed, a thought or a word for the French and British soldiers . . . King Leopold III of Belgium has laid down arms. It is an action unprecedented in history . . . '

A few hours later the fugitive Belgian Premier, Hubert Pierlot (who with colleagues had unsuccessfully tried to persuade Leopold to leave Belgium with them on 25th May) supported Reynaud's denunciation in his own broadcast from Paris. That day, among Allied leaders, only Winston Churchill withheld his condemnation from the Belgian King. In a speech to the House of Commons reporting the Belgian capitulation, he counselled Members to defer judgment until the facts were known. But a week afterwards the British Premier's fairmindedness was to desert him as, in answer to pressure from Reynaud and in the interests of Franco-British solidarity at this grave moment for the Allies, he joined in the chorus of abuse against King Leopold and, in another Commons speech, castigated him for surrendering 'without prior consultation, with the least possible notice, without the advice of his Ministers and upon his own personal act'.

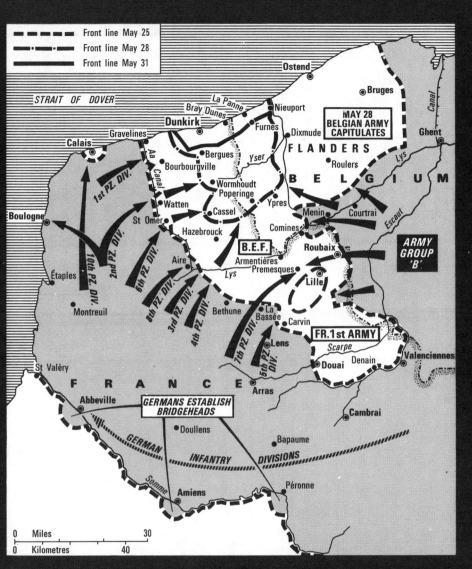

Legend:
- Front line May 25
- Front line May 28
- Front line May 31

STRAIT OF DOVER

Ostend

Bruges

La Panne
Bray Dunes
Nieuport

MAY 28
BELGIAN ARMY
CAPITULATES

Ghent

Dunkirk

Gravelines

Furnes

Dixmude

Canal

Calais

Bergues

Yser

FLANDERS

Roulers

Aa Canal

Bourbourgville

Wormhoudt
Poperinge

BELGIUM

Lys

1st PZ. DIV.

Watten

Boulogne

St Omer

Cassel

Ypres

Menin

Courtrai

Escaut

10th PZ. DIV.

2nd PZ. DIV.

Hazebrouck

Comines

Roubaix

ARMY
GROUP
'B'

Étaples

6th PZ. DIV.

Aire

B.E.F.

Armentières
Premesques

Lille

Montreuil

8th PZ. DIV.

3rd PZ. DIV.

4th PZ. DIV.

Lys

Bethune

La
Bassée

Carvin

FR. 1st ARMY

7th PZ. DIV.

5th PZ. DIV.

Lens

Scarpe

Denain

Valenciennes

St Valéry

FRANCE

Douai

Arras

GERMANS ESTABLISH
BRIDGEHEADS

Cambrai

Abbeville

GERMAN

Doullens

INFANTRY

Bapaume

DIVISIONS

Somme

Amiens

Péronne

0   Miles   30
0   Kilometres   40

Dunkirk—the Allies' diminishing foothold

The great retreat—British and Belgian troops

The churlish treatment of King Leopold who, as Commander-in-Chief of the Belgian Army, allegedly betrayed the French and British by capitulating without warning, makes a sorry story, not strictly relevant to the narrative of the defeat of France except in one respect: Reynaud, aware of the French military blunders that had brought about the present situation, and foreseeing the defeat of France herself in the forthcoming battle on French soil, found in the leader of the surrendered Belgians the perfect scapegoat on whom to deflect the blame for the errors and deficiencies of the French High Command. Militarily, the effect of the Belgian capitulation was, as mentioned, grossly exaggerated; but even if, in the immediate fog of battle, there was room for doubt about King Leopold's precise part in the Flanders campaign, he was later to be totally vindicated of all the charges brought against him, by the testimony of the senior British naval officer, Admiral Sir Roger (later Lord) Keyes, who as liaison officer between the British War Cabinet and King Leopold, was closely associated with the King throughout the Eighteen Days' Campaign and kept a diary recording the King's day-to-day reactions to events, his intentions, decisions, and contacts with Lord Gort and the French High Command.

From this it is clear that, so far from betraying the Allies by not warning them of his surrender move, King Leopold had from the 20th May onwards frequently advised them that, in certain circumstances, the Belgian Army's capitulation would be inevitable. Those circumstances had, in fact, materialized. There was no doubt that Reynaud was prepared for the Belgian collapse. Returning to Paris from London on the 26th after conferring with the British War Cabinet, he was accompanied by Paul-Henri Spaak, Belgian Foreign Minister (he too had briefly visited London) who told him of the King's intention to capitulate, as expressed to a group of Belgian Ministers at a dramatic meeting at Wynendael in Belgium the day before. Lord Gort likewise knew, as he was to admit in his subsequent *Despatch*, that Belgian resistance was virtually at an end – though, in the chaos and confusion prevailing in Flanders on the 27th May he seemingly failed to receive the King's last signal to him: ' . . . He (the King) wishes you to realize that he will be obliged to surrender before a débâcle.'

Much of the trouble in the last dramatic days of the Flanders battle was due to the breakdown of liasion and communications at top level, and conflicting national interests. King Leopold suffered from this probably more than any of his colleagues. Up to the 26th May he was unaware, because no one informed him, that the Weygand Plan had been abandoned. On that day, too, he was the victim of a far worse omission: Lord Gort's failure to advise him that the evacuation of the BEF from Dunkirk had actually started, though on the same date Gort was reproaching the King, whose forces were now in desperate straits, for retreating in such a way as to expose the BEF's left flank. The unhappy truth was that, as the Allied front in Belgium foundered, Allied unity was giving way to the paramount considerations of *sauve qui peut*, and in the search for a scapegoat it was convenient to pin the blame on the C-in-C of the first ally to collapse.

It would be long before King Leopold (about to undergo four years as a German prisoner of war in Belgium, followed by ten months as a Gestapo captive in Germany and Austria) would achieve any sort of vindication and the historical record of events in the Belgian campaign be corrected. If Reynaud and Churchill were never fully to make an *amende honorable* towards the King, at least General Weygand, initially one of his fiercest attackers, was to alter his judgment.

Grim aftermath of Dunkirk

In his book *Recalled to Service* (1952), he says: 'On May 27th the Belgian Army was in a perilous situation. The whole of its forces were still too far from the Yser for it to be able to take up position there in a reasonable time. Its right wing, threatened with envelopment, could no longer be extricated by the French any more than by the British, whose withdrawal on Dunkirk had already begun. The Belgian Command then evidently regarded itself as abandoned by its Allies.'

On the political level, much of the animosity expressed against King Leopold stemmed from the fact that he did not, as Head of State, flee the country with his Government but remained instead in Belgium to share the fate of his army and people. But it should be remembered that, if the King had left Belgium with his leading Ministers on the 25th May as they besought him to do, the Belgian Army would almost certainly have capitulated at once rather than three days later – thus denying the BEF the vital flank support it needed for effecting the Dunkirk evacuation.

For the French, on the 28th May, things looked black indeed. That evening General Blanchard, visiting the First Army commander, General Prioux, at his command post at Steenwerck, admitted that his army group no longer existed because the Belgians were out of the battle and the British were returning to their island. And early on the 29th he informed Weygand that some French divisions were exposed as the result of the precipitate retreat of the BEF. With one ally defeated and the other in full flight from continental soil, the next stage of the conflict loomed that much the nearer and more certain: the battle of France.

The great evacuation of the BEF from the Dunkirk beaches – Operation Dynamo – was in full swing when the Belgians (at no time informed of it) capitulated. It began on Sunday the 26th with the removal of certain base troops, and two days later Lord Gort gave the general order for withdrawal to the Dunkirk bridgehead. Cautious forecasts that it could last no more than two days, and achieve the lifting of only some 45,000 men, proved totally inaccurate. Continuing for over a week, the Dunkirk operation finally removed from Flanders more than 338,000 troops, including 115,000 Frenchmen. It was a tremendous feat of courage and organisation, achieved in the face of determined enemy opposition; but as Winston Churchill was to remind the British House of Commons on 4th June, 'Wars are not won by evacuations'.

It will be noticed that for every French soldier escaping in the great sea lift, nearly three British troops were saved. This was because, as Weygand himself pointed out, the French, mostly men of the First Army, were initially farthest from the coast. The last stubborn defenders at Dunkirk were in fact Frenchmen: over 26,000 of these were rescued in the final shiploads reaching Dover on the 4th June. But more than 30,000 remained to be taken prisoner – the men of the Fortified Sector of Flanders and the 12th, 32nd and 68th Divisions. Well to the rear of these were the bulk of five other First Army divisions (the 1st Moroccan, 2nd North African, and the 4th, 15th and 25th) which, encircled to the south of the Lys, were on the 31st May making their last stand after battling for seventy-two hours to break through towards Dunkirk. Two days earlier, their commander, General Prioux, had been captured with his staff at Steenwerck. Now, after refusing two calls to surrender, General Molinie of the 25th Division, the senior commander, was to yield at 8pm on the 31st. During the crucial first phase of the evacuation Molinie's force had prevented six German divisions from advancing on Dunkirk. The Germans themselves were to acknowledge their valour; for next morning, in the Grande Place at Lille, two French battalions were to parade with their arms before the German General Wegner.

Of the French units that had been ordered across the Lys and subsequently reached Dunkirk, the story of one, a contingent of the 2nd North African Division, was recorded by its commander, Captain Daniel Barlone. On the 28th May Barlone was at Erquinghem on the north bank of the Lys, without orders and out of touch with divisional headquarters. That evening, therefore, he decided to make for Dunkirk. Through the night he and his men fought their way, with their horse-drawn vehicles, along roads almost blocked with a vast one-way traffic of tired Allied troops, lorries and guns. The chaos was intensified by constant air attacks. By dawn on the 29th Barlone's unit was a dozen miles from Dunkirk. Under heavy German artillery fire, they managed to reach Bergues, entry

point to the inner bridgehead around the port.

With the shelling increasing, Barlone's party pressed on, repeatedly plunging into the roadside ditches that were now filling with water released for the defensive flooding of the Dunkirk plain. After six miles they struck the coast at Bray-Dunes, a small peacetime resort a few miles east of Dunkirk. Bray was a huge park of vehicles and equipment jettisoned by troops on their way to the beaches. Negotiating this, Barlone's men learnt from a French officer that the remnants of the 2nd North Africans were re-forming near La Panne, to the east. As they moved off, the floodwater was slowly rising over the dike-crossed plain to their right. They stared horrified at 'the heart-rending sight of tens of thousands of aban-

Rescue off the Dunkirk beaches

A casualty at Dunkirk

doned vehicles and wandering horses'. On arriving at La Panne, Barlone found that his divisional commander and most of his staff had been captured, leaving the CO of the 13th Algerian Rifles to lead the division. Next morning, at a count of officers and men to be embarked for evacuation, the remaining strength of the 2nd North Africans was found to be 1,250 out of an original 18,000.

At noon Barlone was ordered, with a fellow-officer, to embark 550 men at Dunkirk, nine miles westwards. Just short of the port they ran into increasing confusion: there were no police or signposts to direct them through the wrecked town to the embarkation zone. Sheltering from the severe shelling, they finally received their embarkation orders at 9pm. To reach the quayside they had

to negotiate a half-mile stretch and two footbridges under continued heavy fire. Barlone sent the men forward in parties of ten, in single file. Dunkirk was now a mass of smoke from the burning oil tanks, and enveloped in flames from blazing buildings. Wide areas had been devastated, and everywhere the ground was littered with the debris of bombed houses. Over the port derelict cranes projected skywards. And all the time German bombers swooped overhead, unopposed by Allied fighters. (These, in fact, were doing valiant work farther inland.)

At last Barlone's men – with losses of four dead and several wounded – reached the quayside, only to find that the boats assigned to them had already sailed. Not until 3am next day were they eventually embarked on two small cargo ships. At 8am that morning, 31st May, they steamed

into the haven of Dover harbour.

But for all the courage, ingenuity and determination with which the Allied troops, gallantly aided by the RAF, made the Dunkirk operation possible, there was another saving element, provided by Hitler himself. It was the Führer who called off the armoured divisions from completing the destruction of the encircled Franco-British forces, assigning the task instead to the Luftwaffe. At a top-level military conference at Charleville on the 24th May, Hitler rejected a proposal by General von Brauchitsch, C-in-C of the German Army, for a full-scale armoured attack on 1st Army Group. Declaring that 1st Army Group was doomed in any case, Hitler emphasised that the main task now was to prepare for the next stage of the campaign – on the Somme front and extending to the western extremity of the Maginot

Line. To this end he directed the armoured formations to regroup in the Saint-Quentin area and ordered that the Flanders battle should be finished off by the infantry and *Luftwaffe*.

Why did Hitler, with the destruction of the BEF and French First Army in his grasp, make this so peculiar decision? Soon afterwards he confessed to Kleist that though he might be losing a golden opportunity in letting the British escape at Dunkirk, he did not wish his tanks to become bogged down in Flanders mud. Other explanations he gave were that he was anxious to conserve his armoured forces for the next campaign, or that he wanted to check the state of his tanks before committing them to further action. Kleist himself believed that the Führer had appointed the *Luftwaffe* to liquidate the Dunkirk pocket on the persuasion of Göring.

Hitler gave the *Luftwaffe* its orders on the 26th. Instructions were promptly passed to Kesselring's and Sperrle's 2nd and 3rd Air Fleets. East of Dunkirk the XXXIX Armoured Corps was already halted at La Bassée, and now Guderian's XIX Corps received a halt order as it was preparing to move against Dunkirk from the south. Guderian, offered the bald explanation that the *Luftwaffe* was now handling the Dunkirk operation, had to swallow his surprise and chagrin at this sudden tame ending to the chase he had been so brilliantly conducting since the 15th May.

It was under the shadow of the Dunkirk reverse and of the Belgian surrender that, on the afternoon of the 31st, the Franco-British leaders met in Paris for the first Supreme War Council to be held since the start of the German offensive. The mood was grave: those attending had no illusions about the dangers of the next phase of the battle. Clashing national interests now began to obtrude more clearly than ever. In an answer to a plea by Reynaud for the maximum British support for the defence of the Somme-Aisne line, Churchill stressed the need to keep British troops at home to combat probable invasion. This applied also to aircraft, he added. 'If we are beaten,' Reynaud replied, 'the French Army will have played its part. We have nothing in reserve, neither arms, nor clothing, nor reserves.'

General Weygand had been viewing France's prospects with increasing anxiety since the War Committee meeting of the 25th. He too was highly doubtful that his armies could continue fighting without British aid. Pétain, he found, agreed with him. On the 29th he had proposed to Reynaud that the British Government be asked to send troops and planes. 'I hope to stand on the Somme-Aisne line,' he continued, 'but it is my duty to tell you that I am not sure of being able to do so.' It was at this meeting (attended also by Pétain and Admiral Darlan) that Reynaud had suggested turning Brittany, in the event of the Somme-Aisne line being broken, into a last-ditch French fortress. He had repeated the idea at a War Committee held on the 31st before the Supreme War Council meeting. Weygand, previously not unreceptive to the scheme, now flatly rejected it, saying he did not see what troops and material would be available to man the redoubt.

Meanwhile, as the great Dunkirk operation moved towards its close, Weygand and his staff were occupied on more immediate defence problems. On 4th June the Supreme Commander decided to place, to the right of Besson's 3rd Army Group, a newly formed 4th Army Group under General Huntziger (General Requin's Fourth Army and General Freydenberg's Second Army). There would thus be an army group protecting each of the two most probable lines of German advance – the lower Seine and the plains of Champagne. Besson's group would now extend from the Channel coast to the Aisne north of Rheims, and Huntziger's group would cover as

far as the western end of the Maginot Line, linking with Prételat's 2nd Army Group (manning the Maginot Line itself). To support Besson's and Huntziger's groups, General Georges created two mobile reserve forces, one in each army group zone.

Fierily energetic, Weygand was constantly visiting his army commanders, in whom he expressed firm confidence. He had, notably, something good to say of Generals Requin, Touchon, Frère and Robert Altmayer. But in some lower echelons, according to a British military observer, there was cause for strong disquiet. Reconnoitring with a colleague in the Soissons-Rethel-Rheims (Sixth Army) area on 29th May, Colonel Woodall (British GHQ Military Adviser to Air Marshal Barratt, British AOC-in-C) was disconcerted to find no signs of digging in, no tank traps, no trench system and only rudimentary road blocks. Troops and guns were also scarce. This was in contrast to what Woodall's headquarters had heard

from General Georges, that the Aisne line was 'strongly held'. The lamentable situation was confirmed at General Touchon's headquarters, where Woodall was told that the Germans could easily penetrate the Sixth Army front. The Sixth was 'exhausted', officers said with a shrug, adding that in the hard fighting of the last ten days (in which de Lattre de Tassigny's 14th Division had gallantly defended Rethel) it had lost half its equipment.

At his Les Bondons command post General Georges (whom Weygand had found a changed man since the departure of Gamelin) continued to be satisfied with the army's morale. He told Colonel Woodall on 2nd June that the troops were showing 'a new spirit'. They realised at last, he said, 'that they were faced with . . . the loss of their country'. The spirit of Verdun had been aroused, he added, though he had to admit conditions were less favourable than in 1916.

Whatever the state of the army, the French civilian front seemed only half awake to the country's impending danger, and unable to take advantage of the current lull in the fighting. Defence construction was lagging, with civil manpower resources not fully utilised. On the 2nd June General Besson reported to Weygand that he was handicapped in making tank traps by shortage of men. Meanwhile Reynaud was becoming exasperated at the failure of the General Staff and the War Ministry's Chief of Staff, General Colson, to tell him how many civilians they wanted for defence works between the Somme and Paris. A few days earlier, a British correspondent in Paris had been surprised to note a group of workmen repairing the base of a statue on a bridge over the Seine. These were all signs of France's inability, at this critical juncture, to marshal the national forces for a concerted war effort.

Dunkirk: the last resistance

The battle for France

The last loaded transports had hardly left the bomb-battered beaches of Dunkirk when Hitler, implementing the final phase of his Directive No 13, threw his forces against France herself. As May ended, the German armies had moved south from the battlefields of Belgium and Flanders to deploy on the 200-mile long front along the north banks of the Somme, the Ailette, the Aisne and eastwards to Longuyon. From west to east Rundstedt's and Bock's Army Groups B and A confronted, across the narrow river-line, the remaining active elements of the French Army – about 140 divisions against forty-nine. To lead the great assault were assembled ten panzer divisions – the German Army's whole armoured strength – formed now into five corps of two divisions each. General Hoth's, the most westerly, was to strike between Amiens and the sea; Kleist, commanding two corps, was to advance from the Somme bridgeheads at Amiens and Peronne; and Guderian, also with two corps, was to drive south from the Aisne. To reinforce this formidable array of power, the *Luftwaffe* stood ready on the airfields.

The battle started around dawn on Wednesday, 5th June, with a massive artillery and air bombardment on a 120-mile front from the Channel to near Laon. Then the ground forces moved against the three armies of Besson's 3rd Army Group, Kleist's tanks quickly breaking out from their bridgeheads. Before 8am Weygand had hurried from GHQ, Montry, to Georges command post at Les Bondons, where he watched early developments. He now lost no time in issuing a dramatic Order to the French Army: 'The Battle of France has begun. The order is to defend our positions without thought of retreat. Officers, non-commissioned officers and soldiers... the fate of our Country, the safeguarding of her liberties, the future of our sons depend on your tenacity.'

For the men of Besson's and Hunt-ziger's armies, Weygand's phrase 'without thought of retreat' was meant as no empty cliché. They were literally to fight and die where they stood. This followed from the new tactic, mentioned in Weygand's Order of the 26th May, of defence in depth – the chequer-board or *quadrillage* arrangement of fortified positions like villages or small woods, chosen largely in order to deny the roads to enemy tanks. These strong-points were to be mutually supporting, and provide bases for launching counterattacks. From them, even if bypassed by the enemy, there would be no withdrawal. Against tanks, this aggressive defence plan was a vast improvement on the outmoded linear deployment hitherto favoured by the French. But Weygand's formula relied for its success on the possession of aircraft, armour and reserves with which to counterattack the bypassing enemy forces. (In fact, none of these would be available). Yet Weygand remained unrelentingly insistent that his troops must stand firm in their strong-points, from which, he emphasised, there must be no retreat.

Reviewing the situation with General Besson at his Ferrières command post on the afternoon of the 5th, Weygand was satisfied, as was Besson, that the holding tactics were working. Though enemy infantry had stormed the Ailette on the Sixth Army front, it had not won a dominating foothold. In the Tenth Army sector, on the left, all advances appeared to be checked. But in the centre the position was less reassuring. An armoured sortie from the Peronne bridgehead had reached Roye, twenty miles south. Recording his reactions to the day's events, Weygand later wrote: 'Only one anxious question faced us. Would the intervention of our . . . reserves enable these posts (the strong-points) to be supported strongly enough and liberated by destroying the armoured units that had penetrated our positions? That was the problem of the battle.'

Above and right: The Germans turn south: the campaign's second phase
Below: The enemy at rest

That evening General Besson too was sufficiently worried about the armoured breakthrough to be considering partial retirement. During the night he proceeded to issue orders to 3rd Army Group that Captain Beaufre, of GHQ, Montry, described as 'in formal contradiction' to those of Weygand. Thereupon, at 8am on the 6th, Weygand promptly called a meeting with Georges, Besson and Doumenc at Montry. Beaufre, as he recounts, fully expected Besson to be relieved of his command for opposing Weygand's express instructions. After the meeting, asking Doumenc what had happened, he was amazed to learn that Weygand had conceded Besson's case for a strategic retreat (*manoeuvre en retraite*). As Beaufre saw it, if the *quadrillage* plan were abandoned, the troops would lose all confidence in the role assigned to them, and a rout would start that could only accelerate.

By that evening the situation had further deteriorated. On the Sixth Army front the enemy was pushing towards Soissons and edging forward on the plateaux south of the Ailette. In the central Seventh Army zone the German tanks were for the moment contained outside Peronne, though more were being brought up. Here a resolute bomber attack, by Besson's entire 50-strong force, had broken the threat of a further advance. But on the Tenth Army front (Besson's left flank) Hoth's two Panzer divisions had pushed on to Hornoy, twenty miles southeast of Amiens. For Weygand and his colleagues, studying the Montry operations maps, the truth was now uncomfortably clear: with the Ailette crossed and the Somme forced along much of its length, Besson's two wings were giving way.

At 6pm Weygand ordered the withdrawal of 3rd Army Group to a line well back from the river-line from which there was to have been no retirement. In a bid to boost the morale of his hard-pressed troops, many of whom, already bypassed and surrounded, were battling on stubbornly in their 'hedgehogs' with no hope of relief, he foreshadowed a repetition of the chequer-board tactic farther back, 'in order to be ready for fresh successes'. But the brave words could not conceal the fact that by the end of this, the second day of the Battle of France, the French Army was in retreat and Weygand's plan in ruins.

As the German advance gathered momentum, the French began to fall back in growing disarray. On the 7th, Rommel's 7th Panzer Division, one of Hoth's group, raced forward to reach Forges-les-Eaux, twenty-five miles from Rouen on the Seine, threatening to cut off the left formations of the Tenth Army (the IX Corps and the British 51st Division). Late that night Paul Baudouin, informed of this in Paris by Weygand's Chief of Staff, Colonel Bourget, passed on the news in trepidation to Reynaud. The Premier seemed stunned. Baudouin tried to reassure him, but he noted in his journal: 'I know, I am convinced, that the battle is lost.'

Next day Rommel drove on southwest towards Elbeuf, to complete the splitting of the Tenth Army and command a one-hundred-mile stretch of the Seine from Vernon to the sea. In the centre the Seventh Army was dropping back to a point within fifty miles of Paris. Weygand then directed it to cover the capital's eastern approaches as far as the Ourcq. By that evening of 8th June, for the troops of Altmayer's and Frère's armies, and for a newly created formation, General Hering's 'Army of Paris', there was one urgent task: to hold the lower Seine and the defences around the capital.

Again, as at the breakthrough on the Meuse, enormous havoc was being wrought by the enemy Stukas, which everywhere ranged unopposed among and behind the French lines. Weygand, travelling on the 7th towards Rouen to confer with Altmayer, had seen for himself the chaotic results of the systematic bombing of the Tenth Army's communications. 'The aircraft had a free field,' he complained wrathfully. But formidable as was the German assault in this great new southern drive, this time it was, in places, no walkover. The French troops had never fought more courageously during the whole campaign. Many formations were encircled as they stood firm in their strong-points and fortified bastions – formations like General Mordant's 16th Division (Seventh Army), three regiments of which were over-run south of Amiens by Kleist's Panzers. Surrounded artillery units fired over open sights, and the 19th Reconnaissance Group carried out valiant but useless counterattacks, only to be swamped by the enemy's 29th Motorized Division. By the 7th June Mordant's division had been reduced to three artillery battalions and four infantry battalions out of twelve. Against increasingly overwhelming odds the French battled on for two days more.

As the situation worsened, a wave of despondency ran through the higher commands. In the streets of Forges-les-Eaux Captain Beaufre had observed, on the 7th, staff officers firing up at enemy planes with a sort of 'angry resignation'. At General Georges' Les Bondons command post he noted next day the fatalistic mood of the officers manning the telephones. By contrast one senior officer wept openly as he surveyed the operations map.

Four days after the Somme assault fell Hitler's next blow: the attack on the Aisne front. Now, to the right of Besson's 3rd Army Group, the French Fourth Army (Huntziger's 4th Army Group) was plunged into battle. Weygand promptly sent out what he called 'a supreme appeal' to his armies. In a fresh Order he said: 'The German offensive is now launched along the whole front from the sea to Montmédy. Tomorrow it will extend to Switzerland. The order remains, for each one, to fight without thought

General Hoth, commanding a German Panzer Group

of giving ground . . . where the Command has placed him. . . . We have come to the last quarter of an hour. Stand firm.'

France's increasingly grave military position had had serious political repercussions. The rift in the Cabinet between those who wanted to fight on and those who sought an early armistice was becoming wider. When the Germans had struck on 5th June, Reynaud had been trying to strengthen the 'fight-on' party by reshuffling his Cabinet. He knew that the aged, pessimistically–inclined Pétain, so gladly recalled by him three weeks before, was the leader of the defeatist group, closely backed by Weygand, who now took the gloomiest view of the French Army's prospects. While the Premier realised that he could not, for the sake of national morale, openly quarrel with or dismiss either, he decided to get rid of other doubtfuls, such as Daladier (currently Foreign Minister) and the pro-Italian De Monzie (Minister of Public Works). His most notable addition to the Cabinet, as Under-Secretary for War, was that aspiring, clear-sighted professional soldier who had originally brought him a proposal for a French armoured corps in 1934, and since then often discussed military and

More Allied prisoners

BELGIUM

Meuse

Longuyon

Neufchâteau

4th ARMY GROUP (Huntziger)

Montmédy

Aisne

St. Dizier

Sedan

ARMY GROUP A

PZ GROUP GUDERIAN

XLI PZ CORPS

Vouzier

Attigny

Marne

Rethel

4th ARMY

Châlons
June 12

Château-
Porcien

XXXIX PZ CORPS

Rheims

Troyes
June 14

Damery

Epernay

Neufchâtel

Sambre

Aillette Canal

Laon

6th ARMY

Montmirail
June 12

Romilly

June 9

Péronne

Ourcq

Château
Thierry

Seine

Sens

ARMY GROUP B

PZ GROUP KLEIST

XVI PZ CORPS

XIV PZ CORPS

Soissons

Villers
Cotterêts

La Ferté
Sous Jouarre

Roye

7th ARMY

Noyon

Montdidier

Compiègne

Noisy-le-Sec

Amiens

Avre

Oise

Sarcelles

Pierrefitte

XV PZ CORPS

Abbeville

Somme

Hornoy

Corbeil

Paris
June 14

3rd ARMY GROUP (Besson)

Quesnoy

10th ARMY

Pontoise

Forges-les-Eaux
June 7

Les Andelys

Dieppe

Rambouillet

Chartres

Vernon

Dreux

St. Valéry-en-Caux
June 12

Rouen

Louviers

Evreux
June 13

Elbeuf
June 9

Seine

ENGLISH CHANNEL

Argentan

Le Havre

Caen

- - - Weygand line (June 4)
········· Front line June 10

·· · Weygand lin[e]

0 Miles   20   40   60   80
0 Kilometres   40   60   80   100   120

other affairs with him: 50-year-old Charles de Gaulle, commander of the newly formed 4th Armoured Division.

De Gaulle had a taste of Weygand's views when visiting him at Montry on the 8th. The Supreme Commander forecast that after the Germans had crossed the Seine and the Marne, it would be the end. He added that then England would not wait a week before requesting peace terms. De Gaulle tried in vain to argue with him. Equally disquieting, he found various officers at Montry convinced that the battle was lost and contemplating a cease-fire. So unsuited did de Gaulle now consider Weygand to continue as Supreme Commander that on returning to Paris he suggested to Reynaud that he be replaced by General Huntziger. Reynaud made a non-committal response.

Another major problem was then worrying the French Premier: France's crying need for British aid. After Dunkirk, with Britain girding herself against Hitler's expected invasion, that aid had of necessity been almost entirely cut off. In the first days of June, French appeals to London for military and air support had doubled. Despite Britain's own shortages, and the enormous losses of material she had incurred in Flanders, Churchill and his War Cabinet had done all they could to help with troops and planes. But still Reynaud was not satisfied. On the 8th he cabled Churchill: 'My duty is to ask you to throw all your forces into the battle, as we are doing.' Largely responsible for Reynaud's attitude was General Weygand. He had long cherished a grudge against Britain, seemingly for her failures to bear her share of Anglo-French sacrifice in wartime. He now became abusive on the subject at War Cabinet meetings, clashing more than once with General Sir Edward Spears, who was present as Liaison Officer between the British Cabinet and Reynaud.

More pressingly each day, the War Cabinet meetings were dominated by one question: what would happen if France lost the present battle? On the 6th June Weygand, after outlining the position, asked Reynaud bluntly: 'Are you going on with the war? And with what, if the Paris area, which contains seventy per cent of the war industry, is captured?' Reynaud's reply included a reference to the Breton redoubt. Weygand was sceptical, repeating that he could promise no defence in Britanny. Pétain, spectacled, civilian-suited, white-moustached, a pale shadow of the great leader who had saved the French Army in the First World War, usually said little at these meetings. But now he offered the stark verdict that if the present battle were lost France's only course would be to treat with the Germans. In this the old Marshal was not without supporters. That night at dinner the parliamentarian Chautemps (President of the Council) declared to Paul Baudouin that the fighting must stop before France was destroyed. 'Marshal Pétain sees the position the clearest,' he added.

Pétain now believed the fall of Paris inevitable. He stated as much to Reynaud in a paper read at the Cabinet meeting of the 9th. He also pressed for the seeking of an armistice. Reynaud strongly opposed such a move. As the tense discussion continued, Weygand walked in, with reports of the Aisne attack. Painting a bleak picture of the fighting, he said that he believed his armies 'were coming to the end of their strength'.

The situation was indeed becoming precarious. From north and west the Germans were pressing towards Paris. In five days they had driven forward from the Somme and the Aisne to reach, at some points, within fifty miles of the capital. At 10am on the 9th isolated enemy spearheads were poised to cross the Seine. In the forest of Compiègne the famed 'Iron Division' of Nancy (the 11th) was fending off enemy attacks while Frere's Seventh Army fell back to the Oise. Not far to the southeast Touchon's Sixth Army

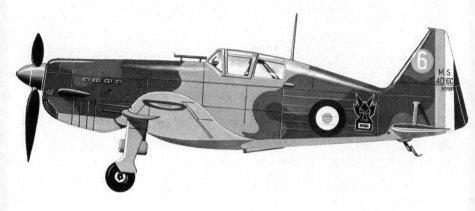

Hawker Hurricane Mk 1

Although the Hurricane was the numerical mainstay of RAF Fighter Command in the Battle, it was already being replaced by the Spitfire as Britain's first-rank fighter. Well able to deal with the ME-110, it was usually outclassed in combat by the ME-109. *Speed:* 336 mph. *Max range:* 443 miles. *Armament:* eight 303-inch Browning machine-guns

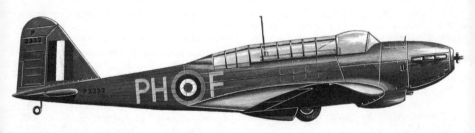

The Morane-Saulnier MS 406
In large-scale service with the French at the beginning of the war and
at the time of the German onslaught, The Morane-Saulnier MS 406 fighter
was no match for the latest versions of the Me-109 serving with the
Luftwaffe. *Engine:* Hispano-Suiza HS 12Y, 860 hp at 13,100 feet.
Armament: One 20mm Hispano-Suiza cannon and two 7.5mm MAC machine guns.
Maximum speed: 304 mph at 14,700 feet. *Climb rate:* 9 minutes 3 seconds
to 19,700 feet. *Ceiling:* 32,800 feet. *Range:* 447 miles at 13,100 feet
at maximum speed. *Weight empty/loaded:* 4,177/5,610 lbs. *Span:* 34 feet 10 inches.
Length: 26 feet 10 inches

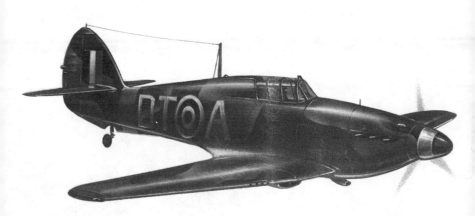

The Fairey Battle
Although it was obsolete at the beginning of the war, the Fairey Battle
was used in considerable numbers in France, and was flown with the
utmost gallantry by the light bomber squadrons of the RAF in that country.
Totally outclassed by German aircraft, large numbers of Battles were
lost in combat. The first two VCs won by the RAF during the Second World War
were won by men flying Battles. *Engine:* Rolls-Royce Merlin III,
880 hp at take-off. *Armament:* Two .303-inch machine guns and up to 1,500 lbs
of bombs. *Maximum speed:* 257 mph at 15,000 feet. *Climb rate:* 8.4 minutes
to 10,000 feet. *Ceiling:* 25,000 feet. *Range:* 1,000 miles at 200 mph.
Weights empty/loaded: 6,647/10,792 lbs. *Span:* 54 feet. *Length:* 52 feet 1¾ inches

was fighting to hold Villers-Cotterets. And, east of this, the big new Aisne assault was developing, of which the initial weight, between Neufchâtel and Attigny, was being borne by de Lattre de Tassigny's 14th Division and Klopfenstein's 2nd Division. At first these stubbornly resisting formations gave little ground, but before night the Germans would pierce the 2nd's left flank to gain a bridgehead at Château-Porcien.

All this Weygand had before him as he studied reports late that evening at GHQ, Montry. He now felt that the time had come to warn Reynaud in uncompromising terms of the eventualities facing the French forces. 'The events of the last two days of fighting,' he wrote in a memorandum to the Premier, 'make it my duty to warn the Prime Minister that the definite rupture of our lines of defence may occur at any moment.' He then outlined various possibilities. 'If this should happen,' he went on, 'our armies would continue to fight until their forces and their resources are exhausted. But their scattering would only be a matter of time.'

That night, events on the Aisne front were underlining the gravity of Weygand's memorandum. Across the Aisne bridgehead at Château-Porcien, Guderian's 1st Panzers were following the infantry storm-troops, and early

on the 10th tanks and infantry would thrust forward as far as the Retourne river (south of and roughly parallel to the Aisne). These, however, would be held late that afternoon by a counter-blow from 4th Army Group's reserve formation led by General Buisson. Meanwhile the 2nd Panzers would likewise follow across the Aisne, to drive south for Rheims, which that night would be threatened with capture. To the east of the 6th, Requin's Fourth Army was now already outflanked and would pull back to the Marne. By the night of Monday 10th June, less than two days after its start, the battle of the Aisne was lost.

Even before the Aisne assault, the dangerously swift German advance had forced on Reynaud a far-reaching decision. On the afternoon of 8th June he had notified the Council of Ministers that the Government would leave Paris for Touraine. Next day at 9pm the decree was confirmed at another meeting. That night at the Elysée Palace, President Lebrun, who had presided at the meeting, reflected on the historic stand of the French Army at the Marne in 1914, and wondered uneasily if the army of 1940 could make a similar miraculous recovery.

Round-up in a French village

Above: German artillery in action. *Below:* Captured French Moroccan troops

Above: The hapless civilians. *Below:* Rommel with Allied officers at St Valéry

Paris falls

For the newspaper correspondents covering the war from Paris, Monday 10th June had a certain wry significance. It was the first day since 10th May that they never received their customary morning briefing from the War Ministry spokesman, Colonel Thomas. Assembled in the clock room at the Quai d'Orsay, the pressmen awaited Colonel Thomas with growing impatience until his non-appearance was explained. Along with a host of other officials the colonel had left Paris. The Government's evacuation of the capital had begun. All day and into the night the exodus continued, as the Government convoys rumbled out of Paris, heading southwest for their destinations in and around the old city of Tours. Despite the alert of 15th May, which might have prepared officials, the evacuation seemed to

have surprised everyone. Few Ministries had made any plans. Civil servants now strove confusedly to improvise the packaging and removal of their files. The difficulties of the evacuation were increased by the need to conceal it from the public as long as possible. Trouble was also caused by the sudden decision to evacuate by road instead of rail, as planned, which produced an unprecedented demand for trucks.

With this complex problem on his shoulders, Reynaud was again approached that morning by General Weygand, with a reiterated call for an armistice. The Supreme Commander interrupted a conversation between him and de Gaulle by striding into Reynaud's War Ministry office and putting before him the document he had written the night before.

Weygand had been uncertain exactly when to present this to Reynaud, but an alarming report from Colonel Bourget on the Seine position had decided him to submit it immediately. His assumption that the battle was lost was hotly challenged by Reynaud. De Gaulle joined in, supporting the Premier. In the quarrel that followed, the Premier virtually showed Weygand the door. The unhappy fact was that Reynaud and Weygand had now, as the latter put it, 'ceased to speak the same language'. In the ensuing days the breach between them would become even wider.

In these troubled hours a blow struck France which, though not unexpected, was none the less painful: Ciano, Italy's Foreign Minister, announced that as from midnight Italy would be at war with France and Britain. Receiving the news at 4pm, Reynaud quickly broadcast it to the French people in a withering radio address: ' . . . Mussolini has decided to stab us in the back,' he declared. Weygand's reaction, when he heard the tidings at Vincennes, was similar. Italy, he wrote, had intervened to 'satisfy her greed for booty with the minimum risk'. At GHQ Montry, officers listened in disgust to an Italian radio broadcast blaring out a string of speeches, punctuated with cheers and the triumphant chanting of Italy's Fascist song, *'Giovinezza'*. There was no doubt but that this latest setback strengthened the feeling among loyal staff officers in favour of an armistice – in the strict meaning of that word as a cessation of fighting, though with no question of final peacemaking.

The Italian move had clearly been imminent. Since the signing of the Pact of Steel in May 1939, Italy had stood firmly aligned with Germany. During the last month Mussolini, from across the Alps, had watched the Allied reverses with growing satisfaction and a mounting confidence that the moment had come for Italy to move in and reap the spoils of an easy victory.

Reynaud, realising the situation, had at his meeting with the British War Cabinet in London on 26th May proposed that an attempt be made to buy off Mussolini by making her certain concessions involving Gibraltar, Malta, Suez and other politically contentious areas. The British had not favoured his suggestion. In Churchill's opinion, the Allies could offer nothing he would not be able to secure by a German victory. So, over

Below: The invader watches Rouen burn. *Below right:* Whose triumph now?

the following weeks, the tense situation had persisted, with Mussolini awaiting his moment to pounce.

For Weygand the Italian intervention meant one more urgent defence commitment: the protection of the Franco-Italian border with the remaining six divisions of General Olry's 'Army of the Alps', already much depleted to reinforce the Somme-Aisne front. But in the event he had little to fear from the Italians. Italy was to prove an unworthy foe. In June 1940 she was singularly ill-prepared for war. Her air force, army (which possessed no more than about ten first-line divisions), and navy were all poorly equipped and her fighting men unenthusiastic. She was to launch no large-scale offensive until 20th June, and then it was held along the French advanced line except at Lanslebourg, in the Savoie department, and Mentone, on the Mediterranean seaboard. The main threat to General Olry's reduced Army of the Alps came not from the Italians but

from the southward-thrusting German forces which threatened to take the French in the rear.

Marshal Pétain, meanwhile, had become more than ever convinced that France must seek an armistice. At 6pm that evening he summoned to his office in the shadow of the Invalides his old First World War colleague and friend, General Serrigny, to discuss the situation. Shown a map which starkly outlined the position, the shocked Serrigny asked where France's reserves were. Pétain replied that there were none, adding that the front could continue holding for some three days, providing it was not totally engaged. He told Serrigny he meant to urge the Government forthwith to request an armistice. Accompanied by Serrigny, he left his office with that intention. That same evening, in his room in the Ministry of the Interior, Georges Mandel, the Minister, was talking with the Paris Prefect of Police, Roger Langeron. He was entrusting Langeron and his 25,000 man force, jointly with the Prefect of the Seine, with the heavy role of representing the Government in Paris when the capital came under German occupation.

To complete that day's dismal picture, another exodus was taking place: the withdrawal of French GHQ to positions behind Paris. This had been inevitable since 8th June, when La Forté had been threatened by the German advance, but Weygand had tried to delay the move as long as possible. Meanwhile a location had been prepared at Briare, some one hundred miles south of the capital in the Loire department, and about the same distance east of Tours. By the 9th General Georges had been driven out of Les Bondons and the enemy was pressing on to menace Montry itself. Now, on the 10th, with his forces fighting along the Lower Seine, the advanced position before Paris, and the Marne – the last line of defence north of the capital – Weygand realized that time was

growing short. Further adverse reports received during the afternoon and evening – the crossing of the Seine at some points, the fall of Villers-Cotterets, enemy advances to the Ourcq and the Marne – finally decided him. Late on the 10th he gave the order to leave for Briare; and the whole unwieldy scattered complex of French General Headquarters began to roll southwards. That night, after a last gloomy dinner at Vincennes, the Supreme Commander himself and his staff joined the exodus in a special train.

The enemy's rapid approach to Paris posed the burning question: what of the capital's defence? Was it to be a battle-ground, its boulevards the scene of bitter fighting, its historic buildings exposed to destruction from German bombs and shells? Or was it to be designated an open city, undefended and handed intact to the enemy? Weygand regarded Paris as

Left and below: **The end of French air resistance**

an 'open city' in that it had no defence within its own limits, but was to be defended on the 'advanced position' eighteen miles north of the city. On the 10th he so notified Reynaud, explaining that no defence would be attempted on its rings of old forts, sited nearer Paris. If the advanced position were overrun, he judged, the city would become undefendable.

Nevertheless, up to now no formal announcement about the capital's status had been made. Parisians were wondering anxiously what would happen if the enemy reached the city. Three days earlier, General Vuillemin, C-in-C of the Air Force, fearing heavy air-raids, had proposed the capital's wholesale evacuation. On the 9th, by contrast, General Hering, Military Governor, had broadcast an assurance that Paris would be defended street by street. Reynaud, appealing for aid on the 10th to President Roosevelt, as leader of the powerful and benevolently neutral United States, declared ambiguously: 'We shall fight in front of Paris; we shall fight behind Paris.' Weygand himself had perpetuated the doubts by leaving Hering uncertain of his responsibilities. The lack of clear direction caused the energetic Police Prefect, Langeron, increasing exasperation. For his part he believed Paris would not be defended.

Finally, to clarify the situation, on 11th June the impatient Hering sent his deputy, General Lannurien, to Weygand at his new GHQ at Briare. From Weygand Lannurien then learned that Paris was in fact to be officially declared an open city. That same day General Hering, now appointed to lead the 'Army of Paris' in its withdrawal south of the city, was replaced as Military Governor by the burly General Dentz, commanding XII Corps of the Alsace (Fifth) Army. To Dentz, aided by the Police Prefect and Prefect of the Seine, would fall the repellent task of staying in Paris and handing over the capital to the Germans.

Parisian weeps for his lost city

Paris would, after all, be spared the threat of destruction. Instead, German soldiers would once more, as in 1871, tread its avenues, imposing themselves on the city for an unknown length of time. Military, Weygand's decision was unquestionably correct. No advantage could have been gained by turning the capital into a battleground, except a slight postponement of the final German victory; for already by the 11th June, after a month of unalloyed reverses, the French Army was a defeated force, its disintegration being hastened by each day's fighting.

Since the false alarm of mid-May Parisians had been gripped by growing anxiety. The disquieting war news and the long columns of refugees trekking through Paris from the north had banished all their old optimistic illusions. With the launching of Hitler's Somme assault the fear that had pervaded the capital rose sharply. Parisians themselves began to join the great southward migration in increasing numbers. Shops, hotels, restaurants and theatres started closing. The Government's evacuation, news of which flashed round the city early on the 11th, intensified the exodus, so that in a few days 1,000,000 Parisians had left the capital. The vast procession of people afoot and awheel stretched right across the city. Other refugees besieged the southern rail termini, fighting for places on already crowded trains. The streets were littered with the debris of a great multitude in flight before the approaching enemy.

Such was the momentum of evacuation that the belated announcement that Paris was an open city, appearing on the morning of the 12th, did nothing to halt the traffic. If anything the flow was speeded up. From his headquarters south of the river Roger Langeron, the Police Prefect, watched the massive exodus. Next day he issued a proclamation 'To the people of Paris' assuring them of the loyal services of the police in their coming ordeal. Langeron himself was greatly heartened at this moment to receive a message of support from that good friend of Parisians, William C Bullitt, US Ambassador to France. That day, in a telephone call to the Prefecture, Bullitt expressed his admiration for the bearing and behaviour of the police.

Bullitt's presence in Paris, after the departure of the French Government, was somewhat anomalous. Though he had asked Washington for permission to remain in Paris in order to fulfil a request by Reynaud and President Lebrun to hand over Paris to the Germans, should it be declared an open city, Washington had intimated that he should accompany the French Government to Tours. But as he was given no definite order, Bullitt had decided on his own initiative to stay in Paris and hold himself ready to act as intermediary in the handing-over of the capital and aid the Parisians in any way he could.

By the afternoon of the 13th June, three days after the Government had left Paris, the leading German units had reached the city's outskirts, being reported at Pierrefitte, Drancy, Bobigny, Noisy-le-Sec and many other points. At 9pm the Police Prefecture intercepted a wireless signal from the German High Command ordering the Military Governor to guarantee order during the passage of German troops, and to dispatch envoys to Sarcelles, ten miles north of Paris on the road to Beauvais, to receive surrender terms. After first refusing the order, General Dentz decided to accept, under threat of military action against Paris. As night fell, the last French troops from the evacuated northern front traversed the blacked-out city's outer boulevards on their way south – the weary remnants of General Mordant's 16th Division, the Seventh Army, men who had battled courageously over the last week, falling back from near Amiens to make their final stand on the Oise and Nonette. Paris now lay open to the Germans.

The German occupation of Paris began in the early summer dawn of Friday, 14th June with the entry of isolated units. From then on the great German influx quickly gathered volume until by 8am a seemingly endless column of motorized troops, headed by leather-jacketed motor cyclists, was moving southwards across Paris. At first they seemed to be moving into an abandoned city, but gradually people emerged to watch the march-past in silence. Simultaneously other huge columns were crossing the city. Many Parisians, unaware of the entry of troops, first knew of the occupation of the capital by the sight of Nazi swastikas flying from the Eiffel Tower, public buildings and hotels. Meanwhile, at Ecouen, near Sarcelles, General Dentz' envoy had signed the surrender terms – an act that seemed little more than a formality, for General von Studnitz, commanding the Occupation Army, had proceeded to impose a tight grip on the city even before the signing, by seizing key buildings, patrolling the streets with armoured cars and loudspeaker vans, and policing the main crossings with tanks and machine-guns. He had thus forestalled all potential resistance by around breakfast time.

German officers had called early at the Police Prefecture to warn Langeron to report to General von Studnitz at 11am. Arriving at the general's office in the Hotel Crillon with his colleague, the Prefect of the Seine, Langeron was peremptorily told by Studnitz that if order was maintained and he could rely on his troops not being molested, Langeron would hear nothing from him.

For the Germans this was a triumphal day. To celebrate it they had planned a victory march through the heart of Paris. They had moved promptly into the Place de l'Etoile and there posted light cannon and machine-guns. Then, at 9.45, the German flag fluttered over the Arc de Triomphe, military bands broke into martial music, and columns of troops moved off in an impressive parade down the Champs Elysees. The men chosen for this honour belonged to General von Koch-Erpach's 8th Division (VIII Corps) which as part of Kluge's Fourth Army had experienced fierce fighting in Belgium and France, around Valenciennes and Douai, and had latterly been in action with Küchler's Eighteenth Army on the Somme and Oise, in the drive to Paris.

Anti-aircraft crew await the counterattack which never came

Groups of sullen onlookers watched them as they swung down to the Place de la Concorde. Elsewhere in the city, by leaflet and loudspeaker, the Germans were attempting to win over the population in a studied propaganda campaign. As more citizens came on to the streets, they were struck by the fine physique and excellent equipment of the marching troops. They were also impressed with their correct and even friendly attitude (the Gestapo had not yet arrived).

Much of Paris that day remained a tense and silent town, its people withdrawn behind shuttered houses. Touring the Latin Quarter, Roger Langeron sensed the anxious, apprehensive atmosphere. Meanwhile, in the Place de l'Etoile, the swastika-flagged Arc de Triomphe was drawing Germans like a magnet. All the afternoon they filed past it, photographing it, paying tribute to its Eternal Flame. That evening it became the resort of mourning Parisians, the wives, mothers and old men. And as the 9pm curfew imposed by Studnitz descended, the city, its streets deserted, was wrapped in a gloom it had never known before. A sorrowful aspect of that first day of the German occupation was the suicides it provoked. One such was the suicide of the noted brain surgeon Professor Thierry de Martel, who that morning took strychnine and left a note expressing his inability to continue living under the Nazi domination.

Fight on or seek armistice?

If French leadership was beginning to falter before the Government evacuation of Paris on the 10th June, the process was accelerated after the Government's arrival in Tours. Not only would services and communications have of necessity been badly disrupted by any move, but the limited accommodation in the old city on its twin rivers, the Loire and Chers, was already strained by the presence of thousands of refugees from Paris and northern France, and the difficulties were increased by poor administrative arrangements.

Reception plans were often sadly inadequate. Many departments and living quarters were dotted around outside the town. Some of the requisitioned premises, including châteaux, lacked a direct telephone link. The Foreign Ministry, lodged in an outlying château, had a single line to the local post office. While the

British Ambassador, Sir Ronald Campbell, had sensibly secured a radio set, the French President, in the Château de Cange, twelve miles from Tours, found himself isolated. For Reynaud, housed in the massive-walled Renaissance Château de Chissay near Montrichard, there was only a hand-operated instrument to the local exchange. General Weygand, one hundred miles away in his Briare château, had to rely on a telephone in the bathroom.

The Ministers in their several quarters were handicapped by being widely separated from each other. To attend meetings they had to hurry between the Tours Prefecture and remote châteaux, along crowded and unfamiliar roads, imperfectly briefed on the latest situation, often not knowing where their colleagues were. And now, with the military position swiftly deteriorating, the rift between the 'fight-on' and 'early armistice' factions was widening drastically. Under growing stresses and with time against them (for the army's total defeat might now be only a matter of days), they spent tense hours quarrelling and debating over the fate of France. Almost continuous meetings were held. From the 11th to the 13th the Council of Ministers met five times and the Supreme Council twice. In the latter, the last Franco-British conferences to be held before the French surrender, Winston Churchill was, as always, the dominant figure. He strove resolutely to boost his ally's wavering spirit and pledged that in all circumstances Britain would continue the fight.

On the 11th Reynaud urgently summoned Churchill to an inter-Allied meeting at Weygand's headquarters at Briare. With Anthony Eden, Secretary of State for war General Sir John Dill, CIGS, and General Ismay, the British Premier landed at a neighbouring airfield late that afternoon. They drove to Weygand's quarters, the unprepossessing red-brick Château du Muguet, where

Winston Churchill

Lord Beaverbrook

the conference started at 7pm. The French party comprised Reynaud, Pétain, Weygand, de Gaulle and two of Reynaud's staff. General Sir Edward Spears, who was present, described the atmosphere as funereal. The French 'sat with set white faces, their eyes on the table'. The only show of confidence came from de Gaulle. After Churchill had opened on a fighting note, Weygand outlined the military situation in gravest terms. 'It is a race between the exhaustion of the French troops, who are almost at the end of their powers, and the enemy's breathless state,' he declared.

General Georges, who appeared in answer to a request by Churchill, confirmed Weygand's assessment. He reported the loss of some twenty-five divisions since 5th June and said France's fighter strength was reduced to about 180 planes. His gloomy conclusion was that France was at the end of her tether. In the matter of British air support, Churchill explained why the RAF could not be thrown into France's struggle. 'History will undoubtedly say,' retorted Reynaud, 'that the battle of France was lost through lack of aircraft.' The Breton redoubt was mentioned – to be dismissed by Weygand as unworkable. Pétain broke in to declare that guerilla warfare

would mean the destruction of France.

After a brief resumption of the meeting next morning, Churchill, on the point of leaving the château to return to England, spoke to Admiral Darlan. 'You must never let them get the French fleet,' he enjoined. According to Churchill, Darlan gave his promise. Spears then talked in turn to both Georges and Pétain. The two soldiers were openly pessimistic. 'An armistice is inevitable,' affirmed the old Marshal. That morning of the 12th, Generals Weygand and Doumenc surveyed the position with General Georges at Georges' headquarters nearby, to be joined shortly by Reynaud and Pétain. So alarming were the reports now coming in that Weygand instructed Georges to carry out a drastic provisional order he had issued the previous day: to pull back his armies to a line Caen-Tours-the middle Loire-Clamecy-Dijon-Dôle-the forests of Doubs. A glance at the map showed that he was abandoning the whole of northern France. In Weygand's own words 'our last line of defence was cracking . . . The Battle of France was lost.' In this harrowing moment he formed, as he relates, an unshakable resolve. He would shortly ask the Government to conclude an armistice.

Meanwhile, at Tours, anxious

Lord Halifax

Admiral Darlan

Ministers – long without news – were wondering what decisions were being taken at Briare. At least they learned with relief that a Council of Ministers would be held that evening in the President's château. At 7.30pm they trooped into the huge salon of the Château de Cange (some Ministers were late because, in the confusion, they had gone to the wrong château). The usual still protocol was dispensed with. Ministers took their seats at random in two rows of chairs placed along the sides of the room.

Weygand, himself delayed on the crowded roads from Briare, was the last to arrive. Asked to report, he detailed the disastrous battle situation and then proceeded to make his dramatic declaration:

'I will of course continue to resist the enemy, if the Council so orders me. But it is my duty to tell you bluntly that from this moment the fighting should cease. The war is irretrievably lost. On the other hand, as Commander-in-Chief of the army and as a loyal Frenchman, it is for me to maintain order in the country. I am not willing that France should slide into anarchy which always threatens to follow a military defeat. That is why – though it breaks my soldier's heart to say so – I repeat that an armistice must be sought

immediately.'

This bombshell brought starkly into the open the issue that was in all Ministers' minds. Reynaud, the first to reply, pleaded for France to honour her obligations. Even if the army were beaten, he argued, France still had her fleet and her empire. Other speakers followed, all rejecting Weygand's proposal, even though they could not contest the logic of his military reasoning. As the debate continued in the gathering dusk, it became clear that almost every Minister except Pétain backed Reynaud. Reading from a prepared statement, the Marshal asserted that any delay in requesting an armistice would be criminal. In reply, Reynaud reminded Ministers that an armistice would destroy Franco-British unity. When the meeting ended at 11pm all that had been decided was to ask Churchill to come to France next day (the 13th) for consultation and advice on the burning question.

The British Premier landed next afternoon on the cratered surface of bombed Parçay airfield near Tours. With him this time were Lord Halifax, Foreign Minister and Lord Beaverbrook, Minister of Aircraft Production. The **French** Government's disorganized state was shown by the fact that no one met them at the airfield.

They finally reached the Prefecture, to be shown to a modest first-floor room (the office of Georges Mandel, Minister of the Interior, which he hastily vacated, carrying his lunch-tray, when they entered). In this impromptu council chamber the British, a party of ten in all, faced the French, represented by Reynaud, Baudouin, now a junior Minister, and de Gaulle. Despite the informal surroundings, no Allied meeting could have been more momentous. It had before it the life-and-death issue that now grew more pressing with every hour: should France sever her links with Britain and seek a separate armistice, or should she (with the battle of France well-nigh lost) abandon metropolitan soil and attempt to fight on in North Africa?

Opening the proceedings, Reynaud broached a new aspect of the problem. 'America is our hope,' he declared. 'Without her we are powerless.' The French Premier had already sent at least two appeals for help to President Roosevelt. He now said he would send a further, more urgent plea. France's sole chance of victory, he asserted, depended on America's prompt entry into the war. He turned to Franco-British relations and bluntly asked Churchill if Great Britain would release France from her promise. The burden of Churchill's reply was that as Britain was fighting on, she must ask France to do the same. Dissatis-fied, Reynaud re-framed his question: would Britain be surprised if France were forced, on account of her suffer-ings, to ask permission to conclude a separate armistice, while still pre-serving the bond between herself and Britain?

Churchill's response was uncom-promising. Britain could not become 'a consenting party', he said, 'to a peace made in contravention of the agreement so recently concluded'. But, like Reynaud, Churchill was looking to President Roosevelt. Ap-proving Reynaud's proposal for an immediate French appeal to the President, he promised that the British would endorse this with a note of their own. When the conference resumed after a break, Reynaud asked Churchill how the French should approach Roosevelt. Churchill advised a blunt, frank application, requesting all possible help short of an expedi-tionary force. The meeting ended on a tense, uncertain note, with the final decision waiting on the American President's answer. As the British party moved out to drive to the air-field, Churchill murmured to the tall, aloof General de Gaulle, who had spoken little at the conference: 'L'homme du destin (The man of destiny).'

Churchill dispatched his note to Roosevelt – a strong, straightforward statement of the French predicament – that night. Reynaud's message, possibly owing to the confusion reigning at Tours, was not sent until next day, the 14th. In it he said: ' . . . I know that a declaration of war does not lie within your hands alone. But I have to tell you in this hour which is a grave one in your history as in our own, that, if you cannot give France in the coming days a positive as-surance that the United States will come into the struggle within a short space of time, the destiny of the world will be changed. You will then see France go under like a drowning person after having thrown a last look towards the land of liberty from where she was expecting salvation.'

Three thousand miles away in the White House, Washington, President Franklin D Roosevelt had been follow-ing Germany's victorious progress with growing disquiet. Though he was only too anxious to help the Allies – the US being benevolently neutral – he had to contend with his country's strong isolationist element and also face the practical problems of what war material to send the Allies and how to ensure its speedy delivery. By the end of May the Allies' predica-ment was obviously becoming urgent. On the 26th Roosevelt and Cordell

Hull, his Secretary of State, requested the French and British Governments not to let their fleets fall into German hands. Meanwhile Reynaud had been envisaging American intervention on an impossible scale. On 18th May he had had to be dissauded by William Bullitt from personally pleading with Roosevelt to declare war on Germany. Ten days later he proposed to Bullitt that the US Atlantic Fleet be dispatched at once to the Mediterranean.

At the beginning of June France's situation seemed to Roosevelt and Hull so desperate that they decided it was useless to consider sending her material which would almost certainly be seized at once by the Germans. Henceforth, they decided, all the aid that America could provide should go to Britain. Arrangements were made accordingly. But the final and all-committing step she would not take. As Cordell Hull made clear on 6th June, the US would not declare war. Thus, in reply to a strong appeal for military aid by Reynaud, dated 10th June, Roosevelt could offer no more than words of encouragement. His further plea, dispatched on the 14th, could have no better result.

Meanwhile, the Allied conference in the Tours Prefecture had not been the last important meeting of the 13th. A Ministerial Council had been arranged for 5pm at the Château de Cange, President Lebrun's residence. This was to be particularly crucial because, as Reynaud had promised the previous day, Winston Churchill was to attend, to give advice on the momentous armistice question. But at 6 o'clock that evening the President, Ministers and General Weygand were still impatiently awaiting the arrival of Reynaud from Tours, along with the British Premier. When Reynaud's car arrived – without Churchill, who had already left by air for England – there was consternation among the Ministers. The embarrassed Reynaud had to parry angry questions, explaining that Churchill was in a hurry to return home; and the meeting began

in a tense, frustrated atmosphere. Once more Weygand gave his military résumé: German armoured units were driving towards Chartres in the west and Romilly in the east, and the French troops in the centre had reached a state of exhaustion. He forcefully reiterated his demand for an early cease-fire – adding that, before negotiations were started, the French fleet should be sent to North Africa.

Support for Weygand came from Pétain. But, again reading a prepared document, he stressed that the Government should remain in France. 'I shall stay amongst the French people to share their pains and miseries,' he said. 'An armistice is to my mind the necessary condition for the perpetuity of an eternal France.'

'This is contrary to the honour of France,' Reynaud declared. Other speakers intervened, for and against an armistice. The meeting closed at 8.30pm, still with nothing decided. It was felt that Roosevelt's reply, as to how far he was prepared to pledge American support, must be awaited. But whatever the President's response, Reynaud's failure to bring Churchill to the Ministerial Council prompts a pertinent question: would Churchill's presence at this meeting of 13th June, with his fiery assurance that Britain was dedicated to fighting on at all costs, have strengthened the faltering spirits of the French Ministers and affected the future course of events?

Reynaud's last act on this day (the day when Parisians were fearfully awaiting the imminent German occupation of the capital) was to broadcast from the Tours Prefecture an address aimed at Americans as well as Frenchmen. To the Americans he appealed for aid, emphasising what America now owed France. To his fellow-Frenchmen he conveyed a warning of trials to come, spiced with a note of dour encouragement. 'We have always,' exhorted the Premier, 'thrown back or subjugated the invader.'

The crumbling armies

For the more spirited French soldiers the most heart-breaking thing about the enemy's phenomenal progress was the apparently vast supremacy of German manpower and equipment. On 12th June a despondent French officer told a British staff officer at Orléans: 'We have thirty-five divisions. Some hold a twenty-mile front: five miles is the normal maximum. Some are good divisions, but others are bad. What can one do? The Germans have eighty divisions with every superiority in equipment. *Que voulez-vous?*' As the French Cabinet and General Weygand havered and disputed in the turmoil of Tours, this was the dismal picture for too many sorely-tried French units. Nine days after the start of the battle of France, Weygand's armies were retreating in a ragged line from the Channel to Nancy, 220 miles east of Paris. On either side of the captured capital the leading German tank columns were racing south into open, undefended country. In the west they had pierced the Tenth Army positions around Evreux, and in the east they were bypassing Huntziger's 4th Army Group to thrust on past Troyes and Neufchâteau towards Dijon. Farther east still, they were threatening, from the rear, the Maginot Line itself.

Now, ahead of the speeding German Panzers, lay the great river that guarded central France: the Loire. Once more, only four days after its move to Briare (on the river's north bank, fifty miles southeast of Orléans), French GHQ was in danger of being caught up by the approaching battle. On the 14th, therefore, it withdrew another 120 miles southeast, to Vichy. But this was only the beginning of a long southward trek, first to Mont-Dore (Puy de Dôme department) and then to distant Montauban (Tarn et Garonne department). By then it would be a mere shadow headquarters, reflecting the total débâcle that had engulfed the French Army.

As the GHQ convoy headed out of Briare across the Loire, the small town of Gien, five miles off, was being dive-bombed by massed Stukas. The

role of this peripatetic headquarters was now, relates Captain Beaufre, being reduced to little more than asking the military and civil authorities, during its stops, whether they were fighting or retiring. During the journey south Beaufre noted two bizarre incidents: at Vierzon, between Briare and Bourges, a tank commander preparing to defend the town was killed by the townspeople; and later, at Clermont-Ferrand, the garrison troops were ordered to parade in their barracks and surrender while their commanding general escaped on his own.

An impression of the French military chiefs at this stage comes from Lieutenant-General Alan Brooke, back in France since the 12th June as C-in-C of the BEF that remained in France after Dunkirk (some 150,000 men who had not been part of Lord Gort's force in Belgium). Brooke visited Weygand at Briare early on the 14th to consult him on the use of the British troops in Brittany. Weygand, looking 'very wizened and

tired', affirmed that the French Army was breaking up, and that he had no reserves. With Weygand, Brooke then called on Georges, quartered nearby. Georges, 'very tired and haggard, but charming as usual', led them to a large wall map showing the latest situation – and notable for several alarmingly deep German Panzer penetrations, marked in red. Gesturing hopelessly, Georges admitted he had no men, vehicles or guns left.

Considering the employment of the British troops, both Frenchmen agreed that the Breton redoubt scheme was totally unrealistic. Brooke estimated that the British could marshal no more than four divisions, whereas the ninety miles of the projected Brittany front would need some fifteen divisions. Weygand nevertheless asserted that, in pursuance of the Allied Supreme Council's orders, he must make a pretence of executing the plan. The two French generals and Brooke then drafted and signed a directive bringing the British forces into the defence scheme. But this order was immediately abortive, for not only would the French Army be unable to provide the necessary troops, but that night Brooke was to be ordered by London to withdraw the British forces from France, and he himself released from French command.

If the French Army was now breaking under the multiple enemy blows, another casualty (over wide areas of France) was the civil community, as shown by the vast tide of refugees surging south from the northern battlezones. Since the 10th May the traffic had grown steadily, to reach, according to some estimates, 12,000,000. Fleeing in disorder from whole regions, these displaced populations had crowded the roads of France in miles-long columns. It was a mass migration impossible to control, producing chaos in the towns and villages

German engineers replace broken bridge

that lay on its route. These burdened, slow-moving people often suffered ordeals of bombing and machine-gunning far worse than if they had stayed at home. Militarily, the great refugee trek positively aided the Germans by blocking the roads to vital Allied supplies and troop movements. The problem had been aggravated by lack of proper planning, so that when the first fugitives had herded over the French border from Belgium and Luxembourg, local officials had no instructions for dealing with them. Moreover, in places it seemed that German agents were at work, creating needless panic and issuing villagers with false directions.

On assuming the Supreme Command, General Weygand had been dismayed at the congestion these evacuee hordes were causing on the Flanders and Picardy roads, and had tried to restrict them by directing them to certain routes, but this measure had soon broken down under

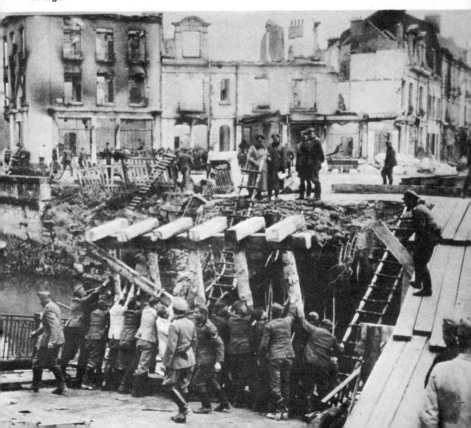

the unmanageable refugee pressure. The start of the battle of France had precipitated another great rout as fugitives from the Seine-Inférieure, Somme, Oise, Seine-et-Oise, Eure, Aisne and Marne departments joined the pilgrimage, many converging on Paris. On 12th June the thirty-five-mile journey from the capital to Etampes was taking twenty hours. Sir Edward Spears, British Cabinet liaison officer with Reynaud, found similar conditions sixty miles to the south, as his car edged its way west from Briare to Tours.

But with the Germans' swift advance towards the Loire, Tours itself was now endangered. So on the 14th June, the day Paris fell, the straggling Government convoys rolled out of the city to their next and last destination - Bordeaux. This thriving provincial capital on the Garonne, 360 miles south of Paris, was the rendezvous not only of the Government but of thousands of refugees.

Congestion here – in a city far enough from hostilities to be considered safe – was worse than at Tours. The fugitive President, Ministers, senators, deputies and officials, along with their administrative apparatus, filled all available public buildings, from the Prefecture and law courts to university and school premises and the Chamber of Commerce headquarters. Every room in the city was taken, and the less fortunate evacuees slept on chairs, in their cars, or even on pavements. So suddenly had crisis overtaken Bordeaux that the uncompleted pavilions of a fair stood abandoned in one of its main squares. Crowds aimlessly roamed the streets, hungry for news. A tense air of uncertainty and apprehension hung over the city.

The atmosphere was worst in those rendezvous that the politicians and their hangers-on had quickly made their own – the famous Chapon Fin restaurant and the lobbies of the city's Hotel Splendide. These spots seethed with rumour and intrigue as, with the armies facing destruction in the north, the ministerial cliques and factions gathered, plotting and jockeying for power in the pro-armistice government that, it seemed certain, would replace Reynaud's within days. From the seclusion of the city Prefecture 69-year-old President Lebrun surveyed these political machinations and noted gloomily: 'The atmosphere of the town is bad.' He was much perturbed at the activities of the defeatists who were buttonholing newly arrived deputies and pointing out the uselessness of continuing the fight, adding that the only thing to do was to end it.

Meanwhile, Paul Reynaud, at his office in the Rue Vital-Carles and in the council room of the Prefecture, was in almost continuous conference, desperately trying to hold the Government together and sustain his 'fight-on-from-Africa' policy. He knew there was no longer any possibility of the French Army continuing resistance, and that it was now a question of how that resistance would be terminated. On this highly touchy issue he clashed violently with Weygand who, tired after a sixteen-hour rail journey from Vichy, called on him on the afternoon of the 15th. Reynaud told Weygand that he wished to stop the fighting in France but would not ask for an armistice, and if necessary would quit France. He therefore suggested that Weygand should surrender with his army like the Dutch C-in-C, offering to give him an appropriate written order. Weygand heatedly declined, saying he would never agree to bring such disgrace on the flags of the French Army.

The dispute was renewed that evening after a ministerial council in the Prefecture. Meeting Weygand in an ante-room, Reynaud warned him that he would have to make a military surrender. Weygand retorted that no power in the world would make him sign the capitulation of an army that had fought as well as the French Army. 'You will do it if I give you the

Above: After the fighting the Germans can relax amidst their conquests.
Right: Fraternisation with the villagers

order, snapped Reynaud. 'Never,' cried Weygand, adding that not a single French officer would accept such a humiliation. 'You are here to obey,' Reynaud rejoined. 'I'm here to defend the honour of the army,' countered Weygand. 'You and the President are trying to evade your responsibility! The Government took the responsibility of declaring war – it must shoulder the responsibility for the armistice.'

Meanwhile, in London, the British War Cabinet was remaining adamant on keeping France to her undertaking, signed on 28th March 1940, not to make a separate peace. Late on the 14th the British Ambassador, Sir Ronald Campbell, visited Reynaud to re-stress Britain's attitude. At the same time, the pro-armistice group inside and outside the French Cabinet were increasing their pressure. At a mini-sterial meeting on the 15th Chautemps (a strong armistice supporter) shrewdly proposed that France should, as an initial move, ask Germany for her armistice terms: if unacceptable, these could be rejected. Almost alone, Reynaud objected – but finally agreed that France should ask Britain's permission to make this request of Germany. In the interim, he advised, the council should await Roosevelt's reply to his note.

But here Reynaud's hopes were to be shattered. Late that night the President's answer arrived. It provided cold comfort indeed. General Spears, who was present when the note arrived, observed Reynaud's air of shocked dismay as he read it. 'Our appeal has failed,' the Premier announced flatly. 'The Americans will not declare war.'

Polite and sympathetic, Roosevelt's note was an unambiguous negative 'May I first of all repeat to you,' it said, 'the increasingly deep admiration of the American people and its

Government for the striking courage which the French armies are showing on French soil in their resistance to the invader.' After remarking that America had helped to equip the Allied armies in recent weeks and would continue to do so as long as resistance was maintained, the note concluded: I know you will understand that these statements do not imply any pledge of a military nature. Congress alone has power to enter into such engagements.'

Reynaud now had no inducement left to counter the demand of the armistice party for an immediate cease-fire approach to Germany, coupled with their refusal to consider the Government's retirement to North Africa. As Weygand declined to sponsor a military capitulation, any armistice request would have to be submitted by the Government. The Premier calculated that fourteen Ministers, including himself, supported this move and six opposed it. He realised, moreover, that if he

himself declined to head such an armistice request and offered his resignation, ready to take his place was Marshal Pétain, backed by the Chautemps group, Weygand, and the sinister figure of Deputy Pierre Laval, who had been busy in the background intriguing on Pétain's behalf.

One Minister who had happily been spared the city's fevered plottings was Charles de Gaulle. As Reynaud gloomily considered France's troubles in the small hours of the 16th, de Gaulle was across the Channel *en route* for London. His mission was to organize British transport aid in the proposed French move to North Africa. In London he was to be involved in a historic but abortive attempt to salvage France from imminent disaster. That morning he met two compatriots, M Corbin, the French Ambassador, and Monnet a Minister and member of the French Economic Mission in London, who told him of a startling plan then being framed for complete Anglo-French

Left: **The Maginot Line proved vulnerable to German dive bombers.** *Above:* **Hitler looks over the captured defences**

Union. Lunching with Churchill, de Gaulle raised the matter with the British Premier who, apparently unaware of the plan, was guardedly interested.

Afterwards de Gaulle and Corbin waited at No 10 Downing Street while the Cabinet discussed the question. The Ministers emerged and told him the plan was being adopted. De Gaulle immediately telephoned Bordeaux to inform Reynaud, who was delighted and asked him to give the wording of the text as soon as possible so that he could submit the plan to a Council of Ministers, meeting at 5pm. 'It was to give me a new argument for keeping France in the alliance,' Reynaud wrote later. In default of troops and war-material, the plan at that crucial moment carried a message of hope and encouragement to a faltering ally. France and Britain, ran the proposal,

should henceforth be a single nation, with joint organs of defence and concerted foreign, financial and economic policies. Much else would bind them at this time of common danger. Finally, the Union would bring all its power to bear against the enemy, wherever the struggle might be.

But imaginative as the British offer was, it was now evident that no kind of Allied intervention could save the French Army from disaster.

For by the 15th June the Germans were driving unhindered into central France. Along most of the crumbling battle front the three French army groups were being steadily fragmented or outflanked. Only on a line south of Paris, where the German pressure was lightest, were the French retiring in any order. On the left the remnants of Altmayer's Tenth Army were being pursued from the Risle (a Seine tributary) due southward towards Poitiers. East and southeast of Paris, where Requin's Fourth Army and part of Touchon's Sixth had virtually ceased to resist, Verdun had fallen and a German spearhead had reached Chaumont, deep in the Haute-Marne department.

Symbolically, the worst blow of all had come in eastern France, with the rolling-up of the 'impregnable' Maginot Line. Caught in the rear, its defenders, the men of Prételat's armies, were in full retreat, menaced with encirclement by German forces that on the 15th June had reached Gray and Vesoul in the Saône valley. The three army group headquarters had been pushed back to points almost as far south as French GHQ at Vichy. General Weygand, returning to Vichy from Bordeaux early on the 16th, learnt all this from Doumenc and Georges at his headquarters in the Hotel du Parc. Georges added that all the senior commanders had emphasised the impossibility of continuing the fight.

For Weygand no doubt now remained. An immediate cease-fire was essential. He flew straight back to Bordeaux, to reach the Prefecture by mid-day, just as the Ministers were leaving that morning's ministerial council meeting. Weygand approached the President, who was standing with Reynaud and others, and told him that unless the fighting ceased at once the army would be totally destroyed. Capitulation, he added, would be against the honour of the flag. Reynaud asked him if, supposing capitulation were included in the armistice convention, he would oppose it as contrary to the army's honour. 'I will tell you that when the time comes.' Weygand answered. The Premier then suggested giving Weygand a written order, thus absolving him of responsibility for surrendering. Weygand tersely declined.

Reynaud had just had a difficult meeting, faced by Pétain, Chautemps and their followers, who were openly resentful of his so-called delaying tactics. To force his hand, Pétain now rose and read a letter of resignation. 'The gravity of the military situation,' he began, '.. convinces me of the need

for the Government to bring hostilities to an immediate end. This measure is the only one capable of saving the country. The enemy advance, if it is not brought to an end, will lead to the total occupation and destruction of our territory.' Having concluded with his offer to resign, the old Marshal made as if to leave the room, with other Ministers preparing to follow him. Reynaud stopped him by suggesting that as Pétain had made his resignation in writing, he should at least await a formal reply. Pétain paused and sat down, reluctantly agreeing to an adjournment of the meeting until 5pm. But he would delay no longer, he said.

At 5 o'clock, two dozen Ministers entered the council room of the Prefecture. President Lebrun took the chair, and Weygand waited in an ante-room. This, as everyone knew, was the crucial meeting. The decision that they had evaded for six irresolute days could no longer be deferred. To emphasise the army's desperate state, during the conference President Lebrun received a message from General Georges at Vichy, timed 5pm. It reported a further worsening of the position and ended: 'It is absolutely vital to reach a decision.'

Reynaud's reading of the latest Roosevelt note produced what Lebrun called a 'somewhat depressing' reaction. Equally discouraging was his announcement that the British refused to agree to the seeking of armistice terms. But most damping for Reynaud was the Ministers' reception – first astonished, then sceptical – of the Anglo-French Union offer. 'Falling like a bomb in the midst of such an unpropitious atmosphere,' wrote President Lebrun, 'it met a very cool response.' Reynaud later noted that he was completely alone in supporting the proposal. Pétain referred insultingly to 'fusion with a corpse'. Tension mounted as Ministers argued about France's obligations to Britain as regards fighting on. Reynaud hotly maintained that France's honour was involved in continuing to fight alongside her ally. Hurling charge and countercharge, Mandel and Chautemps differed violently on the armistice issue. The weary Reynaud now saw before him an irreconcilably divided council. He believed that, even though he had a number of loyal backers like de Gaulle, Mandel, Marin and others, he no longer held a mandate to head the Government. Making a drastic resolve, he therefore rose, formally offered the President his resignation and named his successor – Marshal Pétain.

So, after thirty-eight days of increasingly onerous and thankless leadership in what now was all too plainly a lost cause, Paul Reynaud handed the reins of government to the man whom, ironically, he had called in four weeks before to strengthen his faltering cabinet and stiffen France's will to fight on – the man who had since emerged as the cabinet's peace-seeker.

At 10pm, after a meeting with President Lebrun and Reynaud, Marshal Pétain left the presidential salon as France's new Prime Minister, pledged to end the fighting with an immediate armistice. Pétain had wasted no time: he already had in his briefcase his list of Ministers; and at 12.30am on the 17th June his new Foreign Minister, Paul Baudouin, was in touch with Senor Lecquerica. making the first move towards an armistice request to Germany.

Final defeat

As the battle of France neared its inevitable end, the ordeal of the refugees, like that of Weygand's broken armies, was intensified. One hazard for the fleeing thousands was hunger. Near Mâcon (seventy miles northeast of Vichy) on the 19th June, a mass of fugitives, pushed off the road by advancing motorised units, faced starvation. On learning this General Freydenberg, commanding the remnants of the retreating Second Army, wanted to send a supply convoy north to feed them. He dispatched an envoy to the nearest enemy lines, where he put his request to a general. This officer had regretfully to refuse permission, because next day at dawn he would be needing all the roads in his zone for troop movements. The envoy asked him nevertheless to put the request to a higher echelon, which the general did, though very doubtful of success. The answer came back – a refusal. So Freydenberg was unable to succour his starving fellow-countrymen.

Some of the worst trials were suffered by the refugees who struggled to cross the river Loire. At Orléans, Gien, Sully, the crowds herded on to the narrow bridges to cause huge bottlenecks. Toiling pedestrians were crushed against the parapets by the weight of the wheeled traffic. The confusion was increased by the columns of retreating troops with their lorries and gun limbers. As the bridges were primary German targets, these crawling multitudes were often exposed to German bombing. Under a stream of bombs, terrified civilians hurled themselves into the river, others trampled over the bodies of the dead and wounded. More panic was created by French sappers blowing the bridges. Stopped short at the approaches the procession would then break up in a desperate bid to find other crossings. The mining was done so hastily that it would cut off half a contingent of troops, leaving perhaps the last gun of a battery on the north bank.

Most terrifying was the experience

of refugees trying to cross the bridges of Nantes. (Standing on several branches of the Loire, Nantes had its bridges over each branch). On 18th June a panic flight from the great seaport city was started by a rumour that the bridges were to be destroyed. So dense was the press that the first bridge took an hour to cross. The crowd then battled its way amid massed traffic to the second bridge, frantic to get clear before the explosions. This crossing took another hour. A French officer who was borne helplessly along in the crush later wrote: 'I knew the true face of panic.'

In a disarray that seemed to mark the final collapse of all national order, civilians and soldiers were now swarming down the roads of France together. Mingling with the refugees were thousands of troops, gaunt and dishevelled, in retreat from the crumbling front. Dissolution went even further than this. The rear zones were full of troops who had seemingly not been in action. President Lebrun, travelling from Tours to Bordeaux on the 14th, was concerned to observe the crowds of unemployed soldiers in the towns and villages. At a recent Council of Ministers Weygand himself had admitted that there were some 800,000 men in French camps and barracks, with no arms. Yet at the Riom trials (the Riom Court was set up in July 1940 to try leaders alleged to have contributed to France's defeat) extraordinary allegations were to be made of huge quantities of equipment and material lying unused in the depots – tanks, anti-tank guns, millions of shells. In the free zone of France and in North Africa there were said to be 5,000 aircraft, 1,700 of them front-line planes, of which 2,500 were never flown.

While, in these vital hours, priceless French resources went untapped, the German armies thrust still deeper into the French hinterland. The confused and disconnected reports reaching French GHQ, now at Mont-Dore, completed the story of defeat.

The Germans were speeding down the Channel coast, biting through Altmayer's dismembered Tenth Army to take Cherbourg and Rennes (in Brittany) on the 18th June. Meanwhile the British were hurriedly evacuating their Brittany bases. In the centre the Loire line was broken, and on the night of the 18th-19th Besson's 3rd Army Group began retiring to the river Cher. Eastwards, in the Loire and Saone valleys, German Panzer columns had reached the curving line Roanne-Mâcon-Bourg-Pontarlier, threatening to cut off 2nd Army Group and the Army of the Alps.

Described by Weygand as 'especially poignant', was the fate of the French Third, Fifth and Eighth Armies – the armies of the Maginot Line – isolated by German thrusts in their rear. On the 18th General Georges issued categorical orders to their commander, General Condé, to fight his way out. With its great steel-and-concrete bastion outflanked and neutralised, its potentialities never properly tested, the French Army was suffering a humiliation perhaps worse than if Maginot's legendary wall had fallen to a direct frontal attack. 'It was heartbreaking,' recorded Weygand, 'to have to order our fortress troops to abandon the fortifications which they had prepared to defend with such confidence.'

But by now, further resistance by the French Army had become irrelevant. The previous day, Sunday 17th June, Marshal Pétain, in his first public act as Prime Minister, had broadcast to the French people the news of his own assumption of the Premiership and his move to arrange a cease-fire. '. . . It is with a sad heart,' he said, 'that I tell you today that we must cease the fight (in later versions this was amended to: "the moment has come to try to stop the fight"). I approached the enemy last night, to ask him if he is ready to seek with me, as between soldiers, after the stuggle and in all honour, the means of ending hostilities. . .'

Above: In the communications breakdown that followed the invasion, French refugees eat at communal kitchens. *Below:* A captured fort at Verdun

Frenchmen received the news with shock and grief. Many declined to believe it. Some, in any case, refused to accept it. Admiral Traub, Maritime Prefect of Brest, had placards posted on the town's walls proclaiming that France was going on fighting. At General Alan Brooke's headquarters in Brittany, one of his French liaison officers entered his office and fell into a chair, sobbing bitterly. In London the War Cabinet grimly assessed the implications of this not unexpected turn of events. Churchill hastened to send Pétain and Weygand (now Minister of National Defence as well as Commander-in-Chief) – a warning not to surrender the French fleet to the Germans. In Washington, too, this was a primary consideration. Together with the British, who two days later were to send three senior representatives to Bordeaux – the US Ambassador in Bordeaux, Anthony J Drexel Biddle, Jr, now intensified his attempts to ensure the retention of this precious asset.

Meanwhile Pétain and his new Cabinet had anxiously awaited the response to their cease-fire approach. This the Germans were in no hurry to provide. Not until 6.25am on the 19th did it reach Senor Lecquerica in Bordeaux, in the form of a demand to know the names of the French 'plenipotentiaries'. To make the choice, Pétain, Weygand, Darlan, Baudouin and other colleagues met in the Marshal's office at 9am. Baudouin rather tactlessly suggested that Weygand go himself. Finally, to head the delegation, General Huntziger, highly thought of by Weygand, was chosen. The rest of the party comprised Léon Noel, former Ambassador to Poland; Rear Admiral LeLuc, deputy Naval Chief of Staff; General Parisot, recently Air Attaché at Rome; and Air Force General Bergeret.

At 2pm on the 20th the ten-car delegation, distinguished by its white flags, set off from Bordeaux to Tours, following German instructions that the party was to arrive after 5pm 'on the Loire bridge near Tours'. Firing would be suspended across the Poitiers-Tours road and along the river as the party passed, it was announced. In a final briefing from Pétain and colleagues, Huntziger was directed to suspend negotiations at once if the Germans demanded the hand-over of the fleet or the occupation of French colonial territory.

The surrender delegates' final destination was the forest of Compiègne, some fifty miles northeast of Paris. Theirs was to be a purgatorial journey. Delayed in endless traffic jams caused by the flood of southbound refugees, they failed to reach their first rendezvous, the Loire bridge (about 200 miles from Bordeaux), until the small hours. Meanwhile, their non-arrival had been reported to Bordeaux by the impatient Germans at midnight. From Amboise, on the Loire, they travelled northwards through the night under German escort, without sleep or a proper meal, reaching Paris at 7am. Thence they were driven on almost immediately to Compiègne, to arrive at Rethondes in mid-afternoon, worn out and famished. Hitler had prepared an ironic reception for these defeated Frenchmen: they were to hear their surrender conditions and sign the armistice in the self-same railway coach, drawn up in the same forest clearing, as that in which the Germans had signed the armistice in November 1918, at the end of the First World War.

Near the coach, in its sunlit glade, were a tent for the French delegates and the stone commemorating the Allied victory in 1918. Over it now fluttered Hitler's own standard. The Führer, the Iron Cross decorating his plain tunic, had already arrived with his service chiefs, Göring, Keitel, Brauchitsch, Raeder, and party colleagues, Ribbentrop and Hess. After examining the Allied stone and – as observed by the American corres-

Pointedly, German troops parade before the Verdun memorial

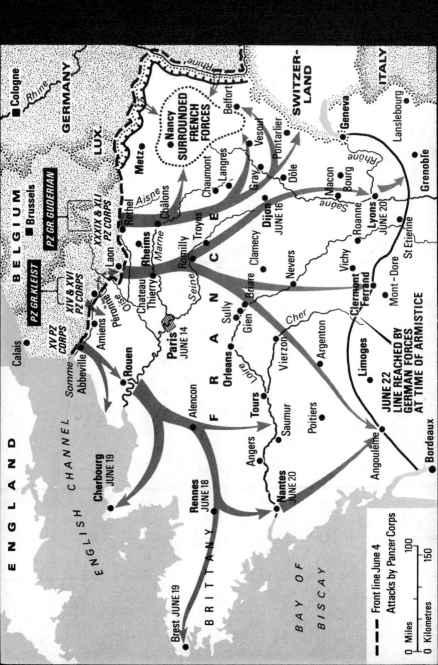

pondent, William Shirer, from behind a nearby tree – executing a little gesture of triumph, he had led the way into the coach. When the French delegates entered, the Germans stood stiffly at the Nazi salute. Then all sat at the long narrow table, Huntziger opposite Hitler.

General Keitel, Chief of Staff of the High Command of the German Armed Forces (OKW) rose and read a brief statement denying German responsibility for the First World War, paying tribute to French fighting qualities, explaining Germany's future aims. When he finished, Hitler and others quit the coach, leaving only Keitel and secretarial staff. Copies of the armistice terms were circulated and each article read out by the German interpreter. No discussion was allowed. The French then retired to their tent to study the text. Curtly informed by Keitel that all queries would be handled by an Armistice Commission, they continued working, with only a frugal meal, until the small hours, when they were taken back to Paris. At 8.30pm Huntziger had been able to telephone Weygand at Bordeaux, reading the twenty-four articles over the poor line and describing them as 'very harsh'. The weary Huntziger added that the Germans were demanding the French reply by 9am next day (the 22nd).

In President Lebrun's quarters at Bordeaux the French Cabinet met at 1am to hear the terms. Many expressed consternation. The shocked President declared them 'unacceptable'. But the Ministers were powerless to do more than suggest a number of modifications. After another meeting at 8.30am these were transmitted to Huntziger at Compiègne, together with the Government's acceptance in principle of the armistice terms. The Cabinet sat almost permanently through the rest of that day, while at Rethondes the delegates were in con-

The end for France — the armistice line is drawn

tinual contact with the Germans, who firmly refused to consider any but minor amendments. They were further hampered by the constant presence of German guards, which allowed them no chance of private discussion. Several times Huntziger telephoned Bordeaux for instructions and advice. An extension on the 9am time limit had been allowed for the final French acceptance, but when this had not been received by 6pm, Keitel sent Huntziger a peremptory order for a reply within the hour. In Bordeaux, Pétain and nine Ministers now gave their unconditional assent to the terms, and Weygand telephoned to Rethondes: 'Order is given to the French delegation under General Huntziger to sign the Armistice Agreement. Report when done. . .'

So, at 6.50pm on Saturday 22nd June, the Franco-German armistice was signed, Keitel subscribing his name for Germany and Huntziger on behalf of France. For the French delegation these last hours had been hard and humiliating, and none had felt the stress more than General Charles Huntziger, representative of the French Army as well as the delegation's leader. Before appending his name, he expressed a hope for better Franco-German relations and said to Keitel in an emotion-charged voice: 'As a soldier you will understand the onerous moment that has now come for me to sign.' Keitel closed the short ceremony with an appropriately soldierly reply.

Forty-eight hours later, in Rome, Huntziger endured the worse indignity of signing France's armistice with Italy – the enemy that had entered the arena only when victory was certain. Fighting was ordered to cease in all theatres at 0.35am on Tuesday the 25th June. After forty-six days of Hitler's main assault in the West, France was defeated. When the cease-fire sounded, the Germans occupied well over half of France, standing on a line that extended from the Atlantic coast at Royan, to Cler-

Left: The Government moves south, and the tricolor is hoisted at Vichy
Above: General Huntziger and M Noel arrive for the surrender ceremony

mont-Ferrand, Saint-Etienne, Tournon, on the Rhone, Aix-les-Bains and thence north to the Swiss border.

What of the cost to France in men and material? The casualties totalled 100,000 dead, 120,000 wounded and a million and a half prisoners. Some 40,000 officers were killed, wounded, missing or prisoner, among the last being 130 generals. (How different a campaign this was from the slogging attrition battles of 1914–18 is shown by the French First World War losses of 1,385,300 killed, 2,675,000 wounded, 446,300 prisoners or missing – a four-year toll which yet left France un-

Below: **An historic moment; the surrender is signed.** *Below right:* **On Germany's day of revenge, Hitler and his service chiefs inspect France's 1918 victory memorial**

beaten.) Losses of equipment and material were immense. German casualties totalled 200,000 of which 40,000 were killed.

Perhaps fittingly, amid this massive defeat, the one zone in which French troops refused to recognize that they were beaten was the Maginot Line. Cut off in the forts of the Maginot Line, more than 200,000 men obstinately continued resisting for five days until ordered to lay down arms by the French High Command.

The 25th June was proclaimed a day of national mourning. In the great cathedral of Saint-André, Bordeaux, the President and members of the Government and diplomatic corps attended a solemn service. That day, too, General Weygand issued to the French Army his last Order. 'The fortune of war,' he said, 'has gone

against us, but at least you responded magnificently to the appeals I addressed to your patriotism, your bravery, and your tenacity . . . Honour is safe . . . Remain united and trust your leaders. Continue to submit to a strict discipline . . . Keep up your spirits, my friends. *Vive la France*.'

Soon after, at three points between Bordeaux and Clermont-Ferrand, Weygand was to review the battle-weary remnants of Besson's 3rd Army Group – the troops of Hering's, Frère's and Touchon's armies. He recorded them as standing proudly, 'with sad faces, but with the steady look of men who had done their duty to the end'.

General Maxime Weygand may have had his shortcomings. Rigid, prejudiced, fiercely authoritarian, a professional soldier to the tips of his fingers, he perhaps carried his loyalty

to the army to extremes. And his intense though blinkered patriotism and profound anti-Communist feeling may have led him to believe that a worse fate could befall France than a German victory. But it was his unfortunate lot to be called in to command an army that was already beaten. Nothing he could have done from 20th May onwards could have materially prevented the débâcle that was already in train. That débâcle stemmed directly from the Ardennes-Meuse breakthrough on 13th-15th May, as a result of which seven-tenths of Germany's total armoured force, opposed only by a frail screen of the French Army's weakest divisions, had been able to reach the Channel coast and roll up the Allies' northern armies almost before Weygand had assumed his new command.

This was a clean-cut military defeat, worthy to rank as one of the classic and decisive reverses of history. Yet, as the military expert, Sir Basil Liddell Hart, points out, 'never was a great disaster more easily preventable'. The German armoured drive, he argues, could have been stopped well before reaching the Channel by a powerful French armoured counterthrust, such a stroke being entirely possible if the French, who had more and better tanks than the enemy, had used their armour in concentrated offensive form instead of as an arm ancillary to infantry, in First World War style.

Sir Basil adds that the German drive could have been stopped earlier, on the Meuse itself, if the French had not hurried into Belgium leaving their hinge (between the Ninth and Second Armies) so weak, or had moved their reserves there sooner. The French High Command, he says, had not only considered the Ardennes impassable but had badly overestimated the time necessary for the enemy to prepare his attack on the Meuse – reckoning that this could not be launched before Day 9, instead of, as actually occurred, on Day 4. Liddell Hart further suggests that the German armoured drive could have been halted in the Ardennes by the use of minefields, or even by the felling of trees along the forest routes leading to the Meuse.

Supplementing Liddell Hart's analysis, the French writer Colonel R de Bardies (*La Campagne 39–40*) sums up, in a wider sense, the direct causes of the French military collapse as follows: absence of the right material and equipment; the wrong training; lack of strong command, as typified by General Gamelin – highly intelligent but wanting the needful force and drive; the dependance on a defensive instead of an offensive doctrine. Beneath these, adds de Bardies, lay a poor national morale and an unawareness of the reasons for which France was fighting.

The Führer greets the news of the signing of the surrender with a jubilant jig

In general, France's military chiefs had clung too long to old concepts and methods, ignoring the revolutionary new war machine, swift and mobile, being created by Nazi Germany. Faced with the ever-present spectre of a traditionally hostile neighbour far stronger than themselves, they had never abandoned the pre-occupation with defence that, apart from a short period before and at the start of the First World War, when outmoded offensive techniques were revived, had persisted since the French defeat in the Franco-Prussian War of 1870. And, for them, defence had meant static linear defence, whether of the First World War trenches or the later Maginot Line. Not until the Western campaign was virtually lost was any serious attempt made to establish a defence in depth. Reinforcing Gamelin's tentative 'kernels of resistance' call of 16th May, on 5th June, at the start of the battle of France, Weygand had ordered the formation of the chequer-board or *quadrillage* defence system; but this had depended on the availability of reserves for counterattack, which by now were non-existent.

For many of her military errors and misconceptions France had to thank Marshal Philippe Pétain, the First World War leader and hero who now, with ironic justice, presided over the French people in defeat. In the immediate aftermath of the armistice Pétain, convinced that France's fate was inevitable, could only counsel his fellow-countrymen, over the Bordeaux radio, to show submission and discipline. It was fortunate for France that another Frenchman had different ideas. Broadcasting to France from London, to which he had escaped on 17th June, General Charles de Gaulle declared: 'We have lost a battle but not the war.' But that is the beginning of another story.

Bibliography

Chronology of Failure: the Last Days of the French Republic Hamilton Fish Armstrong (Macmillan, New York)
Le Drame de 1940 Andre Beaufre (Paris) published in English as
1940: The Fall of France translated by Desmond Flower (Knopf, New York)
60 Jours qui Ebranlerent L'Occident 3 Vols Jacques GPM Benoist-Mechin (Albin Michel, Paris) published in English as
Sixty Days that Shook the West: the Fall of France Translated by Peter Wiles (G. P. Putnam's Sons, New York)
Why France Fell Guy Chapman (Holt, Rinehart and Winston, New York)
A History of Modern France 1871-1962 Alfred Cobban (Braziller, New York)
War Memoirs Vol. 1. The Call to Honour 1940-42 Charles De Gaulle Translated by J. Griffin (Simon and Schuster, New York)
The Six Weeks War: France May 10-June 25, 1940 Theodore Draper (Viking, New York)
The Battle for France 1940 Adolphe Goutard translated by ARP Burgess (Doubleday, New York)
Paris Juin 1940 Roger Langeron (Flammarion, Paris)
In the Thick of the Fight Paul Reynaud translated by J. D. Lambert (London)
The March of Conquest: the German Victories in Western Europe 1940 Telford Taylor (Simon and Schuster, New York)
Recalled to Service: the Memoirs Maxime Weygand translated by E. W. Dickes (Heinemann, London)
The Ides of May: the Defeat of France May-June 1940 John Williams (Knopf, New York)